James Judd

Diary Dottings in Palestine and Egypt

October 28th, 1886, to January 8th, 1887

James Judd

Diary Dottings in Palestine and Egypt
October 28th, 1886, to January 8th, 1887

ISBN/EAN: 9783337119423

Printed in Europe, USA, Canada, Australia, Japan

Cover: Foto ©ninafisch / pixelio.de

More available books at **www.hansebooks.com**

PRINTED FOR PRIVATE PERUSAL.

DIARY DOTTINGS

IN

PALESTINE AND EGYPT.

OCTOBER 28th, 1886, to JANUARY 8th, 1887.

London:
IMPRINTED AT DOCTORS' COMMONS.

1887.

To J. M. Cook, Esquire.

MY DEAR MR. COOK,

These unimportant DOTTINGS were intended for the perusal of those at home, whom circumstances prevented from sharing in the pleasures I have so recently enjoyed. Unfortunately, whilst my caligraphy has been described by partial friends as *picturesque*, by the world at large it is declared to be *execrable;* and as (a caligraphist having no honour in his own household) I regret to say my family share in the latter view of the case, if their pleasure is to be secured, I must necessarily appeal to the art we owe to the intellect of Gutenberg and the enterprise of Caxton.

This being so, to whom can I dedicate these scribblings but to you? To your wise suggestion that an over-wrought brain would find its needed relief in strange scenes and novel surroundings, I owe the last few weeks of travel—to your ever thoughtful and considerate kindness that the time has proved a long delight, and that no care has marred the pleasures of a journey never to be forgotten. To the world you are known as the King of Tourists, as one who has so perfected the facilities for travel, that the enterprise, science, and labour required in their accomplishment are forgotten in the enjoyment of the perfection attained. By-and-by you will be recognised as the great benefactor of your generation, as one who has done more to destroy prejudice, widen our sympathies, and break down the narrow walls of isolation and exclusiveness,—more to make the whole world kin, than any one of the philanthropists of past ages.

To me, besides all this, you are a warm personal friend, whose private virtues and excellences are not few or small because obviously the knowledge of them must be confined to a comparatively limited circle, in which I am happily one. These are reasons sufficient to justify me in inscribing these pages to you, and the fact that you are ready to subordinate your wishes to those of your friends will, I hope, make the dedication not unacceptable.

Ever your faithful friend,

JAMES JUDD.

UPPER NORWOOD,
January, 1887.

Prefatory Note.

I PURPOSE, all being well, to keep a record of daily doings and passing impressions for the dear ones at home. *I would not write a book if I could:* of making of books there is no end. Wilkinson and Lane, Budge and Mariette Bey, Baedeker and Murray, and a hundred others, supply the omnivorous tastes of the many-headed. *I could not write a book if I would:* at fifty-seven 'tis too late to enter the ranks of the bookmaking fraternity. But if I give shortly what strikes me most in countries so sacred and so ancient, it will refresh memory in after years, and possibly be a source of pleasure and interest to those for whom all is written.

October 28th, 1886.

DIARY DOTTINGS.

From London to Gibraltar.

Thursday, October 28, 1886.

STARTED from Liverpool-street Station at 11. My son Walter to see me on board the good ship "Kaisar-i-Hind," bound for Suez and the farther Indies; my immediate friends and companions, Mr. J. M. Cook (J. M. C.), the Columbus of tourists, and Mr. Mortimer Harris (M. H.), the General Manager of the London Chatham and Dover Railway—a splendid vessel of the P. and O. line, not new, but full of all needed comforts, although, after the floating palaces of the Clyde, the "Iona" and "Columba," one is likely to become unreasonably critical. The journey by rail was a short one—to the Albert Docks—but sufficiently long to bring into prominence the contrasts of our social state, and the marvellous differences in appearance and surroundings of the denizens in the East and the West. Surely there will be nothing more marked by way of contrast in the Eastern lands to which I go with the homes of us Western folk, than between the inhabitants of the East and the West of our great Babylon, with their marked and contrasted differences! We left the mooring stage at 12.15 exactly, and, towed by the steam-tug "Victoria," passed the lock dividing us from the Thames at 1 o'clock to the minute. Already I am struck with the strangeness of the new world into which I have entered: the gentlemanly-looking officers, and the tawny, shrivelled, lightly but picturesquely-attired Lascar seamen. We have a large number of passengers on board, some bound for the Gib. only, others whose destination is Malta, whilst the greater number are for the land of the

Pharaohs, or the more distant Indian possessions of the Crown. We sat down to lunch almost immediately after turning our faces down the river. A fair provision : game pie, cold mutton, chicken (of course), and for those who were very bold, and not afraid of *mal de mer*, a *mayonnaise* of salmon. Just opposite us were the Duke of Manchester, Lord and Lady Rosebery, Mr. Calcraft—a friend of the Prince of Wales—and the Earl and Countess of Annesley. Lord Rosebery everybody knows—the coming man say many besides Mr. Gladstone (whose protégé and friend he is), smooth-faced, boyish-looking, about the middle height, with a very pleasing smile and the air of a man who takes life easily, with little envy in his composition and no uncharitableness. Lady Rosebery looks amiability itself, is very stout, and with a little of the accent that is often found with the sons and daughters of Israel. My companion in my cabin—*licensed to carry two*—appears by his luggage to be the Member of Parliament for Carlisle, a Mr. R. Ferguson. I see by my pocket-book that he is a Liberal. We shall not, therefore, quarrel upon political questions if they be broached. I have just had a cup of tea—4.30 p.m.—and hear we dine at 7. There is some probability that we anchor for the night, and if that be so I can write a line to my beloved, with the certainty that a few hours and a postage stamp will take it to its destination. Our dining saloon is at least 120 feet long, lined with cabins on either side with maple-wood doors, and lighted with hanging lamps and side lights at intervals of a few feet. There is nothing very striking in the saloon save its length, but everything is comfortable and the waiting good. I committed a sad breach in the customs of *sea*-good society by calling for the " Waiter," but I shall not err again ; the " Steward " shall receive due recognition for all time to come. 'Tis but fair to say that no response was made to a call so unwonted. I learn we are to anchor for a few hours, so I break off to write my first letter to the dear ones at home. We anchor, Mr. Cook suggests, to give the captain his one opportunity of dining with his passengers. He is a man of sixty, or thereabouts, with a jovial face and white beard and whiskers. He sat next Lady Rosebery and the Duke of Manchester, with the Earls of Rosebery and Annesley on either side. We were very fortunate in our place, as there were some splendid pots of gathered orchids of priceless value, brought from Mentmore or other of the homes of the Rothschilds; we were not so fortunate with the very splendid grapes, white and black, brought from the same place, and had to content ourselves with the poorer sort prepared for us by the P. and O. Dinner was very good, and there was much cheerful talk, and for the first (and I fear the last) time I enjoyed my dinner as at home. A cigarette after, in the smoking-room on deck, and a brisk walk was followed by a game of emasculated whist, nvented, but not patented, by Mr. Mortimer Harris, and specially intended for three. I went to my cabin soon after 10, and slept much better than in the Pullman car provided by the Midland for my Scottish trip. I find my companion is *not* an M.P., but a Mr. Wheeler. Hence Ferguson is, I daresay, a friend, as some of his smaller impedimenta are stored in our cabin. My number, by the way, is 131 ; it is very pleasantly situated and well ventilated—at least it is so now the weather is fine and permits the opening of the porthole. 'Tis the snuggest little place that can be imagined : everything needed : looking-glass and wash-stand, little shelves in odd corners, hooks in plenty, and a curtain that hides our retreat from the outer world, whilst it gives us the needed ventilation and easy access to our fellow-travellers.

Rose at 7, after a cup of coffee brought by our steward, with a biscuit the hardest of the biscuit family. Shown the bath-room, where I had a tepid sea-water bath, and came up for a walk on deck as "fresh as paint." The morning, oh, so brilliantly bright and fresh ! We breakfasted at 9, and soon after passed Brighton. At 11.30 our pilot left us, his trim-built little yacht coming out from Brading Harbour to fetch him home. He is in the pay of the P. and O., and his duties are the conduct of the steamers from the dock to the open channel. We were fairly close to the *Isle of Wight;* saw the houses at Sandown and Shanklin, the Landslip, Snowden Henry's house, and the more personally interesting homes of Ventnor and St. Lawrence. I wonder whether any of the good folks there saw the ship "Kaisar-i-Hind" as she passed the tight little island, or had a thought for those who hung over her side watching the coast line and admiring the beauties of Vectis the fair! We have now quite passed out of sight of land, unless a cloud-like line very far off is the Dorsetshire coast. Our vessel rolls more now that she has not the advantage of the shelter the land affords. Still I am, *so far*, all right, some threatening symptoms having been allayed by a pear of Brobdingnagian dimensions that my kind companion J. M. C. produced from his hidden stores. Had a pleasant chat with Mr. Calcraft and the Duke of Manchester, the latter respecting the Consumptive Hospital and consumptive people generally; mentioned the fact that the factory operatives in blanket manufactories, where oil enters so largely into the working of the wool, are never attacked by this insidious disease. Our lunch-bell sounds at 1 precisely, and, with the exception of the Countess of Rosebery (who is "but so-so," as I learn), all our passengers are in their places. I have just had the ship's barber in my cabin to do for me what I cannot do for myself. He is a yellow-skinned native of the East, and has done his work very well, though I confess I was nervously afraid he would leave me bleeding, the rocking of the vessel being exceedingly unfavourable for sartorial operations of this order. 'Twas very amusing; although my barber spoke English perfectly, our steward, who introduced him, and who is probably a native of Whitechapel or Bromley-by-Bow, would inform him in Hindostanee that at 2 o'clock daily he must present himself in my cabin. No doubt he wished to air his own knowledge of the language of the East, though he was somewhat "taken aback" by the clear English of the barber—"Oh, yes, I understand; I will be here." One is struck with the large number of men on board, all Lascars, save the men in the steward's department; they wash and scrub, and swarm up the rigging, and call to each other in short sharp cries not at all disagreeable, but very novel and interesting. There are large numbers of military on board, who are evidently quite at home; many ladies, wives and daughters of our gallant defenders, and some few nursemaids and babies. I have made friends with one dear little fellow, very much like our *Treasure* at home, and a little *girl* that, but for her sex, I should think was Master Gordon sent out to watch my doings and report accordingly. He looks out from his staring blue eyes with the evident intention to learn all about things in general and me in particular. Before going down to dinner we passed *Start Point*, off Plymouth, the last we were to see of our native isle; from this light we bore away for the Bay of Biscay—bay of terrible import to timid sailors like myself, though I hear that, like other things and people, it doesn't deserve half that is said of it. Of course it is quite dark, and the revolving light shows nothing save itself, as it turns, minute after minute, its brightness upon the waters of the channel. After dinner we took our walk on deck; every minute or two the deep tones of the bell on the vessel's bridge told us when ships were in sight, as well as where they were; one stroke marking the port and two the starboard, whilst three indicated that the vessel was right ahead. All vessels have to carry lights, whose position and colour tell the character of the craft; at the masthead we know it to be a steamer, whilst green and red on the larboard and starboard show it to be a sailing vessel. There are other precautions taken to prevent what all dread so much—a collision at sea; and seeing the risks to which we are exposed, one cannot be too thankful that accidents are so few. A game of whist, this time for four (for J. M. C.'s secretary, a Mr. Kingsford, joined us), prepared us for our bunks at 11.

30. A glorious sunrise, as I saw from the porthole of our cabin: the sun reddening the waters with a crimson as beautiful as ever fancy pictured. Whilst gazing upon its beauties a distant vessel was silhouetted upon its face, pro-

ducing a most singular effect. Soon after bath and breakfast I had my first attack of *mal de mer*, and I fear me much that I can hardly hope to be in a condition to keep up my diary, or care much for what is and may be. There are many modes of passing time besides the general resource of reading, in which all indulge. There is a "sweep," in which most of the men take part, the question being the number of knots the vessel makes in the 24 hours. To-day, at 12, we had run 308, and a young officer, whose cabin is near mine, was the winner ; J. M. C. was nowhere; I did not join. Then there are a kind of deck quoits, bull-board, &c., in which rope-covered iron rings are used. The Bay of Biscay is apparently calm, but the vessel rolls very much, and that I now learn to be the one invariable condition of the Bay, whether waves ride high or low, whether the winds be few or many. I was introduced, with Mr. Cook, to Lord Rosebery by Mr. Calcraft, who, by the way, is a glorious fellow—a kindly, genial gentleman, and one does not wonder that he is a favourite with everybody. I have a shrewd suspicion that a not very distant object of ambition of Lord Rosebery is the Vice-Royalty of India : for this he would be admirably suited—well fitted to follow a man so genial, popular, and wise as Lord Dufferin. We shall see that my suspicion is justified ere long, or I am no reader of signs and tokens. We had a very boisterous night, and as my "trouble" obliged me to lay down all the evening, I slept very little during

Sunday, October 31.

the night, and was glad when morning came. A dose of Eno's Fruit Salt and a warm cup of coffee enabled me to bear my bath and make a show at breakfast. A pleasant chat with Lord Rosebery about West Bristol, Joseph Chamberlain, and Mr. Bright, and a sharp walk on deck prepared me for the Service of the Church, which was read with clearness and solemnity by the captain, and joined in by the greater part of the passengers. Unfortunately, there was no one to lead in the singing, so that the beautiful " Hymns Ancient and Modern," prepared for all, were never used. We are passing *Cape Finisterre* and the coast of Spain, with the picturesquely serrated mountain range. We had passed *Ushant* in the night. The morning is very delightful, and, so far, my first Sunday at sea is beautiful beyond telling. At home I can picture my dear ones returning from church, thinking, no doubt, now and again of the absent rover, who, for his part, is certainly not allowing the novelty and attractions of his surroundings to make him forgetful of those he has left behind. As we have a stiff head wind, we are not doing our 13 knots an hour. M. H. is suffering terribly from the gout; has been obliged to consult the doctor, and cannot show himself at breakfast, though he was with us at the Service, and promises to come down to lunch. The day is somewhat longer and the weather milder than at home, and I stayed out, stretched upon one of J. M. C.'s easy chairs, till after 10 o'clock. Such a glorious night! The stars innumerable and the young moon bright as a crescent sun. At sea one realises the beauty of sunrise and sunset as can never be done on shore. J. M. C. tells me to save my adjectives for Egypt, as there sunrisings and sunsettings are infinitely more beautiful—as different as is the flower from the bud, or the glorious sun from the pale-faced moon. The sails are just now set to gather and utilise the breeze which is rising: they are set and furled by steam power: 'tis strange to see them spreading to the breeze without any apparent agency. We made 299 miles to-day at 12.

Surely never was a finer opening to the most gloomy of months! So brilliant the sunrise, so balmy the breezes. We passed *Cape St. Vincent* at 2 o'clock, and are now fast hastening on to our first stopping place—the *Gib*. All the inkstands are in requisition, as a notice in the grand saloon tells us letters will be collected at the close of the day. My barber is an interesting fellow; his name, he tells me, is *Tom the Barber;* but this I learn is given and taken alike by all the barbers of the P. and O. He has been 15 years on the vessels of the P. and O. Company, has made enough for his simple wants, and is now returning to *Port de Galle*, his birthplace, to spend his days in peace and moderate plenty. We saw one or two whales after passing Cape St. Vincent—my first view of one of these monsters in its ocean home ! Lady Rosebery greatly excited, and everybody more or less interested in the sight. The Lascars are a source of great interest; they crouch on their haunches in a most extraordinary manner, and feed themselves with their fingers from a common pot, the chief ingredient in which is rice. To-day at 12 we had run 311 miles, and having fortunately joined J. M. C. in the sweep, was rewarded with a sovereign as my share of the spoil. It requires careful seamanship to time our arrival at Gibraltar in the light of day ; but for the incoming Governor, who is on board, doubtless we should get there in the small hours of the morning, and see nothing of this interesting protection to the Mediterranean—this little bit of the British possessions ! Well, how little we know what an hour may bring forth ! Just before going to our cabin we saw the captain, and Mr. Cook remarked how many craft we must now look for, approaching as we were the entrance to the Mediterranean. " Never mind their number," was the response, " if only they show their lights."

November 2. A little after 4 I was dozing, not sleeping, when I heard our steam-whistle—in sound like the fog-horn of St. Catherine's —booming out upon the night : then, almost instantly, I heard a sound like the gentle grounding of a boat upon the riverside ; then a crash, and then another and yet another, louder and yet louder. I leaped from my berth, thinking we had grounded, when I heard shouts and exclamations, and in the morning, bright with endless stars, I saw a vessel with all her sails set gliding close by our stern off into the void behind. The vessel, which turned out to be a bark of some 1,200 tons, called the "Still Waters," laden with iron, going north, had collided with us on the port side, carrying away our anchor, a part of the lamp-house, and some feet of our iron-bound bulwarks. The captain followed me, with a rough pilot coat over his night-shirt, and was speedily where I fear he ought to have been before. As soon as we could—and to me it seemed we never should—we returned, swung round, and dropped a boat, which went off to the ship to learn her condition. By this time nearly all the passengers were on deck. Some, on hearing the sound, had supposed we had arrived at Gibraltar, and that, ignorant of our proceedings in such case, we had scraped the pier; others thought it was the result of the careless dropping of the anchor; some, but very few, had slept on, blissfully ignorant of our danger and our escape. We took the vessel in tow, whose injuries were far greater than our own. Her spars were broken, and her sails and rigging destroyed, whilst a huge gap in her bulwarks showed where the blow had first fallen. Strangely enough, though her figure-head was gone her bowsprit remained intact. This delayed us some hours; it was not, therefore, till 10 o'clock that we cast anchor in the Bay of Gibraltar. 'Tis a serious matter; an inquiry is to be held, and we shall certainly not be able to get away to-day. The captain says little, but looks dull enough, as well he may do, for there is no law more fixed than the one that directs a steamer to give way to a sailing vessel, and that visits upon the former, unless there is more than carelessness on the part of the latter, all the consequences of a collision at sea. Certainly, there was no excuse that the morning was hazy, or that the vessel was undiscernible; with all her sails fully set, and her lights burning— for they were burning—she could have been seen even by a landsman's eyes a furlong off. *Gibraltar*, though well known to us by photograph and engraving, is really not easily describable: a great rock, 1,400 feet high, rising up sheer from the sea and from a plain as flat as a dining-table, and presenting, on all sides, heights difficult, if not impossible, to scale; a long and straggling town, lying picturesquely along at the foot of the rock facing the Bay; and crawling up its sides, as far as the skill and ingenuity of man can construct, roads and paths. All this, though more or less common to all places where the mountain backs and the waters front the abodes of men, is here seen in perfection, and gives one a feeling of novelty and marvel that nothing hitherto seen by me in any way approaches.

We went off before the incoming Governor left the "Kaisar." As soon as we anchored he appeared quite another man : he is old, and thin and shrivelled ; and the long grey coat, white trousers, and slouching hat of the voyage, was but the outer covering of the hidden greatness beneath, or, perhaps I ought to say, showed what a poor creature is even the most distinguished of men without the outer evidences of dignity and power. *Sartor Resartus* irresistibly occurs to one's mind, and one remembers that we are all of us naked under our clothes, and that one man is in himself very like another ! In his Governor's uniform, with all his orders about him, one felt he might be worthy to represent our Gracious Sovereign, and uphold the dignity of this great country. We had a carriage, and drove round the town and up to the entrance to the galleries that are the great sight of the place ; they are vast cuttings out of the solid stone, and traverse, with many devious turnings, the Rock on all its many sides, and in which are some splendid specimens of our modern appliances for war and defence, directed out of gaping holes, everywhere, upon bay and sea and land, and which render the entrance to the Mediterranean, shut in as it is by the opposite hills upon the African coast, absolutely impassable to the ships of any nation to which we may be opposed. There are some 1,600 of these guns round and about the Rock, two of them the most recent of our " Woolwich infants," of 100-ton power. The place is very carefully guarded, and closed even against the ingress and egress of its inhabitants after nightfall. We saw great numbers of the monkeys—a very large sort—that abound in the rocks and slopes of the *Gib*. They are never molested, and are as impudent as we know monkeys always are. The market is a large one, and the supplies of fruit and vegetables very plentiful. I was much struck, upon our first reaching the Bay, at the numbers of what appeared to be memorial columns erected up and about the town and slopes of the Rock. Naturally enough one supposed them to mark the scene of some heroic deed or some heroic death ; they are, however, but an attempt to deal with what is a problem everywhere—the efficient treatment of SEWAGE GAS! Well, the good folk have at least the merit of making the external evidences of this striking and somewhat picturesque. I suggested that when asked, as by the way they always are, the object of these pillars, they should reply, "Oh, they are erected to Major Gaseous and General Sewage!" In the afternoon we were the witnesses to a very pretty sight—the people's sympathetic parting with the outgoing Governor, General Sir John Adye, who is unwontedly popular not only with the military (who, by the way, I hear number some 6,000), but with the civilians also. He has shown such interest in their affairs that they feel it to be like parting with a personal friend and benefactor. He was escorted by a troop of a Kentish Regiment that is quartered here—indeed, they lined the road from the Governor's house to the place of embarkation; but the charming part was the earnestness of the people generally. We got down before them, and took up our place on a boat moored off in front of the landing-stage. Sir John was dressed in plain clothes, but his handsome and most benevolent face needed nothing to mark him out as a man among men. Plenty of soldiers, plenty of gaily-dressed ladies, plenty of music, and flowers and favours; plenty of booming cannon and brightly-decked vessels—all the various evidences of love and goodwill with which we are wont to welcome the coming and speed the parting guest. Our ever-thoughtful friend, J. M. C., telegraphed lest some distorted account of our late disaster might reach the eyes and ears of dear ones at home. After doing this we met with the representative of the *Standard*, who was on board, whose destination is Malaga, and who had sent to his great paper a short statement of the collision and of our safety. Before closing the memorials of the day, let me put on record my feeling of gratitude to the One who helps in time of trouble and preserves in the hour of danger—who saved us from what might have been a fearsome tragedy and a great disaster. If happy are the people that have no history, then surely fortunate is the man whose sea voyage is monotonous, and whose diary is devoid of interest and incident. We lie off the town, and the glittering lights and shadowing rock are at once solemnising and delightful ; we smoke our pipes or cigars, leaning over the quiet waters, admiring silently or discoursing eloquently, as fancy or feeling leads us. Whist and our bunks at 11.

November 3. We are still in the Bay. Different hours are stated as the time for our departure. Twelve, we are confidently told by one, whilst 4 o'clock is fixed by another. Some few go off in the boats that are gathered about us, but the uncertainty as to the time for leaving prevents any general exodus. 'Tis a glorious morning, and I am surprised to see no yachts or other sailing boats, but only here and there a steam launch and some smaller boats that ply for hire in the harbour. I hear, however, that it is impossible to have yachts, as the Bay is exposed to sudden and very severe gusts of wind, coming round the point and through the valley dividing the Bay from the Mediterranean. Indeed, several of these sudden squalls come on as we lie anchored here ; they are called *Levanters*. The town is certainly very bright and charming, quite different from one's notion of what a place gathered under the shadow of a mountainous rock is likely to be. I must not forget to mention that here for the first time I saw the tropical trees and plants in high perfection—palms and cacti, orange trees and melons, with their fruit growing and ripening in the open air. A very striking tree is that bearing the seed-pods of our useful condiment, *pepper;* it is much like the acacia, but fuller of leaf, more graceful, and with the red seeds hanging in drooping clusters from its pendant boughs. There is a well-kept public garden, in which is a bronze bust of Wellington, with an interesting Latin inscription, which was translated to us by our cultured companion, M. H. This is the favourite lounging-place of the good people of the Rock ; here the bands play ; close by is the assembly-room—a somewhat pretentious building, and one can hardly imagine a lovelier spot in which to pass time, talk scandal, and gaze out upon the sparkling waters of the Bay and the white Spanish towns that skirt its further shores. There is another view more extensive—that from the Galleries we have visited, facing and dominating the neutral ground and the Spanish territory. Here you see, beating against the farther side of the Rock, the blue waters of the Mediterranean, whilst the bright green waters of the Bay lap the town and strand on the nearer side. Immediately below us, as we gaze over the dizzy height, are the sacred homes of the dead; innumerable upright gravestones mark where the Protestants lie: a smaller space is allotted to the Romanists, on the other side of which is the Jewish graveyard, where the memorials of the dead are all recumbent, like the bodies of those they cover. The sight was saddening beyond expression: not because it reminded one of man's mortality, but because of the cold and bare and bleak surroundings of this God's acre. There is a little churchyard, nestling among trees and near the busy haunts of the men of the Rock, that conveys no such feeling; 'tis the isolation of the spot, and the absence of trees and verdure, that make the sight so painful. Our modern cemeteries are "gardens" of the dead, and surely we leave those we love, amid their pleasant surroundings, with lessened sorrow because of this. We left the Bay at 4 o'clock, and steamed round the point into the calmer waters of the Mediterranean. We had a magnificent view of the *Gib.* on its other side; we see it in all its greatness here—no trees, no houses, no strand—sheer rock, rising up majestically from the sea— nothing to mar its grandeur, nothing to lessen its gloom! After our usual game of whist, we turned in to our bunks, thankful that our enforced inaction was at an end, and that we were speeding on to our destination, with bright stars above and smooth waters beneath.

From Gibraltar to Malta.

November 4 to 6.

THE piano was heard to-day for the first time. Now that the ice is broken, doubtless we shall see of what our passengers are made. Lady Annesley is said to be both vocalist and instrumentalist, and there are others here who will be found able and willing to contribute to our pleasure. *Nothing has occurred worthy of note.* On Friday we had what are called "fiddles" on the table at dinner—square-rimmed trays, fixed, which hold your plates and glass, and prevent the otherwise unpleasant results of the pitching and rolling of the vessel. They indicate *squalls* and their consequent inconveniences. To-day we are as calm and smooth as when in the Bay of Gibraltar. Perhaps I may here give a sketch of the good vessel in which I find myself, and of my surroundings. The ship, the "Kaisar-i-Hind," is one of the P. and O. Company's finest vessels, about 10 years old, of 4,023 tons register, was built at and hails from Greenock, whose busy Scotch town is the extreme northern point of its journey, as China is its eastern. She is well-fitted, but as things now are, a little old-fashioned; she burns 54 tons of coal in 24 hours, when at full speed ; is manned with a captain and crew of some 170 souls, all told, and carries this voyage more than 100 first-class passengers, and some 40 in the steerage. The greater part of the crew are Lascars and negroes from Zanzibar : most of these latter have been rescued from slavery by our ships stationed on the African coast. The wages of the Lascars is from 15 to 20 rupees per month (30s. to £2), and of the negroes from 7 to 10. Our Captain (Stead) is a man of, I should think, over 60, quiet, polite, and the very model of our notions of a true British sailor: stout, tall, strong, and bearded like a pard. "For nearly 30 years," as he said, with a quiet pathos not to be forgotten, "I have been in the service of the Company, in command of their vessels, without a collision or accident, and now it has come.

'Tis only a question of time with us all. There's my old friend Captain ———; it was suggested to him 'twas time for him to retire. But no, he would take one more trip; he took it, and his vessel was stranded on the rocks off *Ushant*. Ah, the pitcher that goes often to the well comes to grief at last!" I pray for my good friend a considerate judge and a good deliverance. The second officer is a short, stout young fellow of perhaps 33, with black hair and close-cut mutton-chop whiskers. He will probably get cashiered in consequence of our collision, as he was in charge at the time it occurred. The doctor in charge of the vessel is not at all like our usual notions of that important individual. He is young, tall, is dressed like a naval officer, has a bright eye, a fair moustache, and a pleasant voice. I should think him to be that dangerous animal, a lady killer, not to be made much of by jealous husbands or particular papas. Besides these and the younger officers—who are "fit as fiddles and smart as paint"— there is a Mr. Liversedge, who is a sort of travelling purser, or confidential general representative of the Company and its interests. He would be, I should say, consulted in any emergency by captain and crew, and by passengers, gentle and simple. I understand he goes from vessel to vessel, as may be required, wherever the freight is especially valuable, either in passengers or money. We owe his presence here to the fact that we have on board a Duke of Manchester, an Earl and a Countess of Rosebery, and a Lord and Lady Annesley, to say nothing of our late companion, the newly-appointed Governor of the *Gib.*, and various lesser dignitaries. I must not forget those who specially minister to my comfort: there is first my cabin steward; nothing could be better than his cheerfully-rendered service. For some day or two he addressed me as Captain Judd, but as I ventured to suggest that my position, if any, in the army entitled me to a much higher title, I am now *Mr. Jude*. Every morning at six hot coffee and a biscuit are brought us in our cabin; at half-past six or seven he comes to tell me my bath is ready; upon my return I find my boots polished, my clothes brushed, everything ready for the completion of my morning toilet. I have already mentioned my barber, Tom. The bath steward is a Lascar, and he does his work in the quiet and noiseless way peculiar to this patient race. Once only there was a mild altercation between him and my cabin steward, which I learnt afterwards was as to whether the bath had not been prepared for His Grace of Manchester (we use the same bath-room, and at about the same time). The dining-saloon steward is in no way remarkable; he never pitches the soup down my back, though now and again he might be excused for doing so; he never keeps me waiting my turn, and, so far as I know, gives me a fair share of the best of the fruit that completes our seven o'clock repast. There is a quartermaster who looks after the comfort of the passengers on deck; he is very much like Gilbert's Joe Golightly in the "Bab Ballads," and I should think was "hipped" and slightly bilious, and given to tell gloomy stories to his mates after the labours of the day. Our passengers are various enough, but, so far as I can see, there are none who are marked by disagreeable characteristics, and that, to say the least, is a comfort; there is no vulgarity, noise, or buffoonery, and no one even distantly repulsive in person or manner. Gen. the Hon. Sir A. E. Hardinge left us at Gibraltar; I have already described him, and need only add that he will have all his work to do if he is to satisfy the "scorpions of the Gib"—for so I learn the inhabitants are called—after a man so genial and popular as General Adye, whom he succeeds. I heard that he is already out of their good books because he failed to acknowledge the greetings of the civilians. They want to know why the wife of one of his aide-de-camps should come with him instead of Lady Hardinge, and why his aide-de-camp, her husband, should be in India whilst his wife is at the *Gib*. Oh scandal, oh envy and all uncharitableness! Why are ye here? Why not stay in May Fair, or at St. Paul's, or Pimlico, or be contented with Jericho or Jerusalem? The Duke of Manchester is a very favourable specimen of his class : tall and

well-shaped, quiet, gentlemanly, intelligent and urbane—
willing and ready to talk and walk with all. He exchanges
his views freely, and is a nobleman well worthy of his
position and of the respect in which he is universally
held. When talking of the Irish question, he spoke of the
painful position of many of the larger life-owners of the soil,
of whom he is one ; of the fact that those who suffer most are
those we are accustomed most to envy—the titled nominal
owners. The estates are almost invariably largely charged with
dowers for widows, and jointures and annuities for the younger
members of the family ; these are fixed and unalterable ; falling
rents affect them not, agrarian disturbances pass them by untouched, but my lord, who is thought so rich, and whom most
men envy and all unite to depreciate and abuse, finds himself
often with little or nothing after the fixed outgoings are provided
for. His remedy seemed to me feasible and just, and one
would think will some day be adopted ; it is to get advances
from the State, upon the security of the property, at 3 per cent.,
with a trifling addition to pay off the principal in, say, 30 years,
and in this way, without loss or danger of loss, discharge the
incumbrances and relieve a class who have certainly some
claims to consideration, if it be only the fact that they belong
to the great human family ! Lord and Lady Rosebery I need
say nothing more about ; whether it be true or not that
" Hannah " brought the youthful Earl three millions of money,
certain it is she brings him a loving and affectionate disposition, which shows itself in her every look. The Earl of
Annesley is a smart looking man of 50, who seems characterless
and common-place, but who may be a worthy upholder of all
the best traditions of the House of Nobles. Her Ladyship is
young and pretty, needs repose of manner, but is doubtless a
loving wife and mother. From the *Gib.*, among other additions,
came Mr. and Mrs. Locke King ; the former I suppose to be the
son of that earnest Liberal, Locke King, who long represented
East Surrey, who died last year, and who was the brother of the
Lord-Lieutenant, the Earl of Lovelace (who married Byron's

"Ada"). He is cold and taciturn. She is lively as a cricket—
a bit of a coquette, I think, and certainly pretty, though with
thin lips (which generally indicate temper), and with a clear
cut nose of the patrician order. Mr. Calcraft is here only for
health. He is the head of the Board of Trade—that is, Chief
Secretary. He is a companion I shall not soon forget. He
does literally nothing, save to perform the ordinary functions
of life—eat, drink, and sleep. He has never read a line since
he started, he told me. I sympathise with him. He has been
overworked, and needs the recreation that idleness and novelty
afford. There are several other men of whom one will ever
retain very agreeable remembrances. There is a Mr. Bunten
and his wife and daughter. He is a great owner of iron mines
in the North, and is on his road to India for pleasure and
health. His wife is the eldest daughter of Mr. Maclure, the
eminent lithographer (Maclure, Macdonald and Co.). He is
very genial, and such a fine fellow; a little deaf, but full of
pleasant talk. He must be a good master and a warm friend. We
have, too, Mr. Scobel and his agreeable wife, and their adopted
daughter, a Miss Southey, grand-niece of the poet. Mr. S. is on
his way to take up an important position as one of the legal
Council of the Viceroy of India, and will be a Privy Councillor
when he gets there. Besides these, I must specially mention
one or two of my immediate neighbours at meal-times.
Immediately on my right sits a Mrs. Wilkie, the wife of
General Wilkie, the Commandant at Cairo, who gained his
early spurs at Inkerman at the age of 17. She is a gentle-
woman in the true sense of the term; not robust, yet fairly
enjoying the sea, and is a great critic of our military policy, and
very decidedly opposed to short-time service. She knows my
political leanings, and although a member of the Primrose
League, is neither shocked by my views nor bores me with
her own. Next to her, on the same side, and therefore within
our circle of talk, is a Mrs. Stokes, on her way to join her
husband at Malta, where he is first lieutenant on the " Dread-
nought," Prince George's ship. She is young and very

pretty, is a Canadian, proud of her people, and, as all young and good wives should be, very proud of her husband. I tell both of my wife, children, and grand-children, and they, while tolerant of my talk, are not, of course, particularly enthu siastic or responsive ! I daresay there are others I shall get to know, but meanwhile I must go on with my general notes.— The collision has a little unnerved me; any sudden and novel noise or commotion in the night wakes me, and the night just past was a miserable one in consequence. We had been talking of rats: Mr. Cook contributed a tale of some on the Nile who stole and stored his dates ; Mr. Scobel of some who played hide and seek with a favourite cat ; and other little bits about these rodents made me, no doubt, dream of them. At all events, I was awakened by what I thought was a rat running over my feet in bed. I dashed out pretty quickly, but returned after an unsuccessful search for my tormentor. I did not sleep for some time, and when I did I was awakened in the same way and with the same result. Whether there was a rat or not I cannot say, but I disturbed my "stable" companion more than he liked, and effectually prevented any further sleep. I am very fortunate in this same companion. It might have been far otherwise. There is a military man on board who, had he been fated to share my cabin, would have made the voyage miserable. He is pragmatical and cantankerous—always talking and always objecting, and that, too, almost invariably with a sneer against those from whom he differs. He is no doubt an intelligent man and an able officer, but he is, I am sure, a martinet, neither loved by his inferiors nor liked by his men. Whether or not, as Sydney Smith said of Lord John Russell, he would be ready at a moment's notice to take command of the British army, lead the Channel fleet into action, and perform an operation for stone, I know not, but I am sure he has a very high opinion of himself, and, like the Spanish statesman, he would tell you that had he been at the creation he could have suggested a thing or two. Or I might have had others equally objectionable, though for other reasons. There is a man I have christened "Corded Velveteens." He has a jacket, which he perpetually wears, made of that useful material, while his head is surmounted with a well-worn stable cap. He is probably a worthy fellow, and I think is kind-hearted, for he has a child on board that he nurses fondly; but his bunk *must* smell of the stable, and I dread to think of what my condition would have been had he been No. 130. My companion is very different, and quite unobjectionable. He is fair, somewhat above the middle height, his age about 28, a little like Adrian, has a queer upper lip, but bright eyes, a neatly-trimmed beard, and is careful in his attire without a suspicion of foppishness. He is well read, can cap my quotations, and prefers substantial literary pabulum to what is trashy and ephemeral. We have long and very interesting chats about things in general, and I find him, what is so pleasant in the young, light and jocose without frivolity or buffoonery, sparkling without froth, and bright without bitterness, not too serious but never irreverent or profane. I shall carry away pleasant memories of my cabin companion, J. V. Wheeler. I have not mentioned a Mr. Ferguson, who is with the Earl and Countess of Rosebery; he is very nice; is tall and fair—reminds me of Norman—is 28, I am told, though he certainly does not look more than two or three and twenty. He is the member for Leith Burghs, was Lord Rosebery's private secretary, and, though he will probably never make any great mark in political life, will be a universal favourite, and share in the future advancement and honours of the belted Earl, his warm friend and present companion. There is another young fellow, tall, thin, and smooth-faced, and, despite his somewhat attenuated legs, dressed in cycling suit with knickerbockers complete. He has taken all the prizes at school and college, has passed most creditably his examinations in Hindostanee and Persian lore, and has obtained a minor Government appointment at Kurrachee. He is a great enthusiast, an optimist, and has faith in a kind of sublimated Christian pantheism, that is to be the universal religion of man. He believes the seeds of good exist everywhere and in everybody, but that they can only be fanned into active life by the unselfish efforts of men ; that those who are disposed to help in this Divine work must give up themselves absolutely, contract no family ties, and, whilst interested in the home life of others, must seek none for themselves. The ever-present wants and wishes of wife and family, as he convincingly argued, must prevent that devotion to the interests of others which is imperatively required if the world is to be duly served and saved. So far as he was himself concerned, his desire was, whilst fulfilling the duties of the position he is about to assume, to give himself up absolutely to the good of mankind, and to use his means and his mind in the work in which his whole heart is interested. His life must needs be solitary and his old age lonely, but there will be compensations and rewards for him beyond the reach of others, which will amply repay him for any seeming loss. I felt deeply impressed by such generous and far-reaching views in one so young, and pained and humiliated that, despite my many years and much experience of the sorrows of man, I was still selfishly interested in the narrow circle of family and home. I regret to say, however, that before very long I found my young friend preferred other society to mine—that of the Miss Gordons, Miss Bunten, and other agreeable young ladies on the "Kaisar." Once or twice he abruptly turned the conversation when I ventured to express my entire concurrence in his views upon the clogging effect of family ties, or expressed my admiration of his intended solitary life. This indisposition to pursue the old subject of talk became so marked that, after one or two attempts, I gave up my young philosopher. Very soon after this, on a bright starlit night, I was startled, but not surprised, to find that one of a cooing couple, sitting under the shadow of Lady Rosebery's deck cabin, was my young friend sworn to celibacy, talking to his companion in "accents sweet and low." I hastened away, but not before I heard, if I mistake not, his well-known voice quoting, in subdued tones, but with considerable emphasis, the notable lines by Lord Byron :—

"Maid of Athens, ere we part,
Give, oh give me back my heart!"

Whether he got as far in this somewhat amorous poem as—

"By that lip I long to taste;
By that zone-encircled waist,"

I know not, nor can I tell what the result then might be, but I have no doubt, if I watch the Indian press, I shall see, despite his enthusiasm for humanity and a solitary life, that he has joined the family of the Benedicts. I must not forget, by the way, two others of our fellow travellers who have helped to make our journey exceedingly pleasant—Mr. and Mrs. S. S. Howland, of New York. They are what are ever the most agreeable of all companions—cultivated Americans; intelligent, receptive, full of talk, most appreciative of all good things, without a suspicion of pride or the least suggestion of egotism or self-assertion. Mrs. H. is the daughter of one of the millionaires of America, a Mr. Beaumont, the American partner of the great house of Rothschild. They are, of course, on the most intimate terms with the Earl and Countess of Rosebery, the Earl and Countess of Annesley, and all the other great people of our company. She is evidently delighted with M. H.—his puns, his jokes, his quotations, his almost universal knowledge, have made both husband and wife his friends for ever. She comes down to watch our game of whist, and although she affects to take me under her patronage, and to sympathise with my mistakes and misfortunes, it is quite clear to me, as to J. M. C., that it is M. H. and his witty talk that attract her to the board of green cloth. Mr. Howland has given me his card, pressed me to visit him in America, and has promised to go over our works in London. They are delightful people, enjoy life thoroughly, and have no want unsatisfied — save that they have no children. Ah, well! the blessings of life are fairly apportioned. With all their riches, I wouldn't exchange places nor give up my dear ones for all the wealth of the Rothschilds! I must not attempt to say anything about my two immediate companions, J. M. C. and M. H. If I said what I feel, my Diary would look to any strange eye perhaps a little fulsome; if I said less, I should myself be dissatisfied. Mr. Cook, so kind and thoughtful, so considerate for the weaknesses he never shares, so untiring in his ministries for the present and his plannings for the future; and Mr. Harris, the Admirable Crichton, the wit and scholar—who breakfasts with Horace and sups with Virgil—with an intellect as bright as that of a cultured man of thirty, and a store of " wise saws and modern instances " that can only come with years and experience; with a power of appropriate and ready quotation that suggest the combination of the best qualities of Brougham, Sydney Smith, and Macaulay—a classic, a linguist, a poet, a philosopher—show me, ye gods and little fishes, the equal of my friend M. H.!

7. I was on deck to see the sunrise and our run into the Quarantine Harbour at Malta, where we dropped anchor at 6 o'clock. Before we moored, Lieutenant Stokes was on board, a bright young fellow of about seven-and-twenty, a little like the Duke of Edinburgh. He had to wait for his wife with what patience he could, for, as another lady shared her cabin, she was invisible for a full half hour. I watched them off the ship with a good deal of interest, and with the sympathy we all have in the meeting of lovers, whether married or single. I can't and shan't attempt to describe *Malta*. Gibraltar is 1,300 miles from London, Malta 2,280; it has a civilian population of 155,000, and the military number 6,500—only a few more than the garrison of the *Gib*. We are just an hour before Greenwich time, so that when we are six o'clock with the sun shining you are five o'clock with the gloom of night still about you. *Valetta* is the chief town of the island; it is certainly very picturesque, and as it is the first of the places connected with St. Paul's travels and the scene of his shipwreck, an indescribable feeling comes over me as of the scene of some previous stage of

existence, of some world in which long ages ago I was an inhabitant and bore my part. Perhaps the remembrance that 'tis the Sabbath day—that it was St. Paul's Melita—that it is a scene of sacred story—may have helped the weird feeling referred to. However, the strangeness as well as the beauty of the surroundings, and the novel sights and sounds that speedily met us, brought me back to the newness and the life of this important possession of the British Crown. First we saw seven great coal barges slowly towed to our side by a wheezy little harbour launch, with some 40 or 50 begrimed Maltese lying upon their black freight. Then we were surrounded, almost as by magic, with at least a hundred boats, with their singular half-Venetian prows, bearing vendors of fruit and a thousand trifles to tempt the traveller,—some of them for the purpose of taking the passengers off to the town that we saw rising above the ramparts and bastions of the place. We did not land, however, till after breakfast, which for this time only was prepared for us at 8 o'clock. Meanwhile there came along a boat containing a singular crew. A fierce-looking fellow (with the barest of clothing, with eyes that attracted, repelled, and frightened you) used the oar, which is worked like those of Venice, the oarsman standing erect; with him were three others, all, as Tom Hood says, with "no clothes to speak of." One was a little boy with closely shaven head, of 7 or 8, whilst the other two were perhaps 18 or 20. "Me dive, sir! me dive, sir; throw th' money, me dive, sir!" and I saw at once that these were the men whose dexterity we have all of us heard of—who plunge in after sixpences, catch them long ere they reach the bottom, and bring them up in their teeth or between their toes, to the astonishment of those who have never seen the sight before. There were telegrams and letters for Mr. Cook and for some other fortunate passengers, but no one was allowed to leave until after the visit of the quarantine officer, who came out to us with his yellow flag flying directly we dropped anchor. We landed about 9.30, escorted by two of Mr. Cook's representatives, one of whom knows half a dozen languages, and is the head of the important offices established here. We had two carriages; in the first was the Duke of Manchester, Mr. Cook, Mr. Calcraft, and Mr. Harris; in the second, myself, Mr. Kingsford, and the gentleman I have mentioned. I hadn't the best company, but I had the best guide, and was shown all the sights and had all the novelties explained as could hardly have been done by anybody else. The town is well paved; that is, there are no unmetalled roads; but they are abominably irregular, and we were here and there jolted almost out of our seats. The place is suggestive of the Moorish and the Italian, and here and there are glimpses of bare and stony acclivities, with occasional shrubs, which show what pictures have told me are the characteristics of the Holy Land. We went to the Palace of the Governor, the Library, the Market, and to several of the most notable of the churches. The scene most to be remembered was the view obtained from a garden terrace not far from the Governor's Palace, which opened up to us a sight of the greater harbour and of the Mediterranean fleet lying here under the supreme command of the Duke of Edinburgh. He is very popular, as is his Duchess. His palace is one generously vacated by the Governor for his accommodation; it is, perhaps, two or three miles from Valetta, and is large enough to enable the Duke to keep up a show of state, somewhat in accordance with his position and dignity. Maltese society is proud of the Duke, and though, of course, the old Maltese nobility, descendants of the Knights of St. John, are at feud with the English upper or official class, I hear that the Duke and Duchess fairly hold the scales, and succeed in pleasing—with now and again some difficulty—both the social camps. At the recent levée some 600 attended, and nobody could say it wasn't representative, for I was told by Mrs. Wilkie, with a little touch of indignation, that there were townspeople there whose place was to serve, not to be waited upon—who were dependants, not equals! The children are squalid and dirty; the men, dark-looking creatures, badly clothed, but by no means slothful; the women ugly as harridans, repulsive as sin. All have "expressive purple eyes," but are otherwise very unattractive. The native women of the middle-class wear a very singular head-dress, made of silk or other black material, on one side like a much-extended old-fashioned poke bonnet, and with a long sweep of material on the other that can be drawn round the face and over the chest. Malta owes everything to the P. and O. vessels and the other lines of steamers that call here, and the passengers they bring. I was told that the money spent in Malta by these visitors is estimated to be at least £70,000 a year. Well may the people welcome the coming, if they do not speed the going, of the great steam leviathans that make here their bi-weekly call. The most interestingly repulsive place visited by us was the Monastery of the Franciscans, where we were taken into the crypt and shown the skeletons of the dead monks in niches, in the clothes they wore at their death. They bore tablets stating their name and age and date of death. One was marked as being 110 years old. There was a good deal of ingenuity shown in the disposition of the figures. Some had their bony hands clasped meekly across the breast, some their hands uplifted as though passionately appealing to their audience below, some with upward look as though gazing into the Heaven above, and some with bowed head as though sinking under the weight of age and infirmity. Strange as it may seem when speaking of dressed skeletons, there was marvellous and distinct character in each of these ghastly remains of humanity. The bodies are prepared by a slow baking process, and, I believe, the monks still continue thus to dispose of their dead associates. The Church of St. John is a magnificent building ; it dates from 1570, and has been recently restored ; the pictures in it are of no great value, though they profess to have a Michael Angelo. After our sight-seeing we went to lunch with Mr. Cook and his friends Mr. and Mrs. Royle. They are very charming people. He is the representative of the P. and O. Company at Port Said, a great merchant, a barrister, and I know not what beside, and I would venture to say that in each and every position he acquits himself equally well. His wife is tall and fair and most interesting, whilst their sweet little girl must be a dear source of pleasure and anxiety to the fond parents.—I was very sorry to be unable to drive to the creek into which the toil-worn sailors steered the ship that bore the God-led Paul. I hear there is a pillar erected to mark the spot. How different must be the scene now to what it was when Paul, saved by the centurion from the swords of the guard, landed with the crew, "some on boards, and some on broken pieces of the ship," and found a hospitable though "barbarous" people to receive them. I read the 27th of Acts with new delight, and enjoyed as I had never before done the graphic account of the perils of the sea in the days when Rome ruled the world. We left about 5 o'clock, steaming out into a choppy sea that speedily sent me to the side of the vessel to suffer and to moralise.

———>◆<———

FROM MALTA TO PORT SAID.

mber 8.

EARLY in the morning we passed "a certain island called *Clauda*," and skirted the long and diversified coast line of the Island of *Crete*. Again I felt myself where the sacred shut out the profane, with a profound thankfulness that I had been permitted to see the scenes of the past with which one's Bible and one's faith are ever identified. I always see the sunrise, which I do very lightly clad. This precedes my bath; my shave follows, and then, if the ship doesn't roll too much, I get half-an-hour for my diary. To-day a little chaffinch came on board; it must have travelled quite 300 miles, for we were that distance at least from land. Poor little thing ! it is so tame, it nestled up to one of our lady passengers, and is greatly petted of course. We have had several visitors of this order, but none whose journey had been so long.

November 9. Lord Mayor's Day! I wonder whether my good wife will go; with whom, and how the day will pass! A telegram at Malta informed us that the Socialists had abandoned their intention to join the procession, and would content themselves with a meeting in Trafalgar Square, so there is no fear of any "bother" in the streets of the City. At dinner Lord Rosebery drank to me as the representative of the City, coupling my name with that of the Lord Mayor; and I replied by drinking the Prince of Wales's health, coupled with that of Lord Rosebery. Now that we are nearing our destination, when many of us must part, we are getting very friendly and social.

November 10. My dear wife's birthday! May God in His mercy bless and keep her to be the living, loving wife and mother until my race is run, and I sleep with my fathers! The first time since we were boy and girl together that we have spent this day apart from each other. I am writing this before the sun rises over East Knoll, though here he has been shining for some two hours in all his glory. The weather delightfully balmy and pleasant. How unlike the fogs and frosts of England! Towards the end of the day we passed from the beautiful blue into first the green and then the dingy and perturbed waters that show where the Nile empties itself and discolours all. The coast line—long and low—has been for some time seen by us, and, preceded by blue lights from our ship, and rockets from on shore, about 7 o'clock we anchor inside the breakwater at *Port Said*, and I behold the land of the Pharaohs, and the entrance into—so far as results are concerned—the mightiest of the many works of engineering skill that our day has seen —the *Suez Canal!*

November 11. Coaling, that most horrible of afflictions, was soon over, but the cleansing of the ship continued, it seemed to me, a great part of the night. No bath, no barber, no pleasant walk on deck—everything in turmoil and confusion. A somewhat sensational notice, signed by the doctor, advised passengers not to go ashore, as virulent small-pox prevailed, and informed us that no pedlars would be permitted on board. We learnt that the notice was made as forcible as possible at the request of Lady Rosebery. If her ladyship's purpose was to prevent her husband from leaving, it failed, for the first among the few to land was Lord Rosebery himself. The scene was very striking; not, however, because of anything in the land, which was characterless enough, but from the many-coloured garbs of the people and their unmistakable Eastern appearance. We were to take off some 60 or 70 passengers from the "Nizam," one of the P. and O. boats coming from Venice and Brindisi, among them being the Duchess of Manchester and the Lady Alice Montagu, her daughter. The vessel did not arrive till 3 o'clock, so there was plenty of time to watch the moving scene around us. No words can tell of the wondrous activity prevailing everywhere: vessels of every tonnage and from every country passing us for the Canal; nearly opposite us, with the quarantine flag flying, was a large screw steamer of some 3,000 tons burden—the "Africaine"—whose living freight consisted of some 1,500 pilgrims returning from Mecca. Such a strange appearance they presented, with their long grey sack-like coats, cowled like monks! They pay about £2 each for the journey from the Red Sea, supplying themselves with their simple food. I am told, and can readily believe, that 'tis a sadly pestiferous cargo, and the sufferings of the poor souls terrible. Among the many good deeds done, and to be done, by Mr. Cook, which will make him a national benefactor deserving a niche in the temple of fame, none surely will rank so high as the work he has undertaken in connection with this annual pilgrimage of the followers of Mahomet. They are now pillaged and poisoned—a large percentage never return to their distant homes, but feed the fishes of the seas and whiten the shores of many a desert land. Although the Canal, nearly 100 miles long, owes its existence to the skill and enterprise of a Frenchman, and though its funds were raised by our Gallic neighbours, its revenue is derived from English shipping mainly—more than 82 per cent. of the tonnage passing through its narrow channel hailing from English ports, or being owned by English merchants. We all know something of the character of this work, and of the enormous revenue—more than a million per annum—derived from the tolls levied for the use of this 95 miles of water-way, but one needs to be here to see what it really means. Immense vessels, flying every flag, and laden with passengers from, and with all the produce of, every land, pass to and fro with startling rapidity. 'Tis a splendid port, and 50 sail of the line, I am sure, might ride at anchor in safety within its sheltering breakwater. Several of Mr. Cook's agents were on board as soon as morning came; two of them men to be noticed anywhere: long-robed, turbaned, dignified, tall, and stout. Mahommed, the favourite of everybody, smiling, alert, obliging—Mrs. Cook's friend, evidently madly in love with that excellent lady, for when I told him she had mentioned his name, and desired to be remembered to him, he took both my hands in his, said she was a dear lady, and blushed from olive brown to Nubian black. We stayed on board until all the passengers were transferred from the "Nizam," had lunch, and then parted from the companions of this part of our journey—the greater part of them for ever! Lord Rosebery came to the ship's side to bid us farewell, and, with the warmest good wishes of others, we rowed ashore. The parting from Mrs. Howland was a serious trial to our friend, M. H.; that he wiped his manly eye more than once, that he was absent-minded and taciturn for a full half-hour after we left the ship's side, is no reflection upon his manhood, but is further evidence—if any be needed—that the greatest men have points in common with the smallest, and share in that "one touch of nature that makes the whole world kin." We separated here—myself and Mr. Kingsford for the hotel, Mr. Cook and Mr. Harris for Mr. Royle's (whom we left at Malta), where we all dined in the evening. The hotel faces, or nearly so, the quay, and is in the midst of all the life of the place. Port Said, 3,215 miles from London, is the creature of the Canal; and its population is mostly European. It is built upon a narrow spit of land reclaimed from the desert, and lives by the trade that comes with the travellers to the East who make it their halting-place. There are no carriages or horses, and the means of locomotion for the people are donkeys, and for traffic with other places in the desert, the camel. Our dinner was very perfect, and though I heard complaints of the cook from the *locum tenens* of our host, it seemed to me we had the magnificence of the East with the dishes of the West. Lord and Lady Rosebery and Mr. Calcraft lunched here earlier in the day, and if their lunch approached the excellence of our dinner, then they had no reason to regret the repasts at Mentmore and Park Lane. The captain of the "Nizam" dined with us. He is a good-looking man, but chiefly notable for a nose of the Wellington type. Mr. A. W. Haydn and another gentleman, whose name I forget, are very pleasant, gentlemanly, cultured, and in every way worthy representatives of Mr. Wm. Royle : they made our evening most agreeable and ever memorable. They told us strange tales of the late Sultan, and much that was interesting about the present and the dethroned Khedive. At night I made my first acquaintance with a mosquito-curtained bed, but I regret to say the continued blowing of foghorn-like whistles by the incoming and anchored steamers and craft in the Port, and the never-ceasing barking of the dogs, prevented the possibility of sleep. A new law comes into operation on the 1st of January, I learn, to prevent the unnecessary blowing of the whistles, but I hear of no Sir C. Warren who shall relieve Port Said of its dogs.

From Port Said to Jaffa.

12. CAPITAL breakfast at the hotel. Thanks to Mr. Cook's thoughtfulness, I am not left to the inanities of Port Said. He leaves for Cairo, whilst I wait till Saturday afternoon for the vessel that is to take me to Jaffa for my

Palestine trip. He suggests, and I eagerly fall in with the suggestion, that I go with him and his party as far as *Ismailia* in Mr. Royle's steam launch, and return alone in it to Port Said. Delightful journey. We (*i.e.*, Messrs. Cook, Harris, self, Kingsford, General and Mrs. Wilkie—the General met his wife here—four agreeable Americans, with Mahommed and two other of Mr. Cook's staff) leave about 11 o'clock for *Ismailia*, which is about half-way through the Canal, lunch on board during the journey, and get into the Desert immediately after leaving Port Said. On our right are the shallow waters of the Lake Menzaleh, swarming with fish and birds; the red-breasted flamingoes in immense flocks, wild ducks, and other valuable denizens of the air who love the water and find their sustenance there. General Wilkie tells me the Egyptian Government derives an income of £70,000 a year from farming this valuable water mine. Port Said is supplied with water from the Canal of Sweet Waters at Ismailia, and we see by the side of the Canal the pipes that bring that essential article to the people of the Port. I saw with intense delight, for the first time, the living representation of poor dear Benwell's "*Star in the East*," so far as camel, rider, and guide are concerned: the slow long stride, the mounted rider, the walking Arab, and the desert sand, all brought the picture vividly to mind. On the left we saw, too, the mirage, the fanciful presentment of distant waters and islands and verdure. The "Serapis" passed us on its return from India, and innumerable other vessels, large and small. Nothing could possibly be more interesting, though the outlook is monotonous. Ismailia is situated on the right of the Lake Timsah, the lake that saw all our transports gathered before the great battle of Tel-el-Kebir. There is room for the whole British fleet in this lake, and its sudden appearance after our long journey through the narrow Canal was very startling. This was the scene of the festivities presided over so regally by the late Khedive, on the occasion of the opening of the Canal. A kiosque overlooking the lake, built with every Eastern adornment, and approached by avenues of palm trees transplanted for the day, was the gathering-place of the representatives of all European and most Eastern peoples on that historic occasion. A little further on, embowered in feathery trees of the tamarisk order, was the palace erected for the use of the Empress Eugénie. The cost of the entertainment is altogether estimated to have reached nearly three millions sterling ! Really, the more one hears of the magnificence and generosity of Ismail, the more one regrets he was not retained as the connecting link between the old and the new, between Eastern prodigality and barbarous splendour and Western civilisation and the economies demanded of European life. Ismailia is exceedingly attractive. The place was planned by the genius of the Canal, Mons. Lesseps, who has a villa here ; the roads are all at right angles, and are planted with a kind of free-growing acacia, with their long hanging pods of bean-like fruit. Here is the Canal of Sweet Waters which supplied our troops in their early campaign, and which, as I have said, gives the people of Port Said the only fresh water they possess. There were some very interesting discoveries of ancient stones and statues made when digging here, the hieroglyphics upon which show that one of the Ptolomies had planned a canal, upon lines not unlike that of the great Frenchman, more than two thousand years ago. Verily, there is nothing new under the sun ! I did not reach my hotel till after 11, where, alas ! the same causes as before prevented me from sleeping, with the added troubles of eczema and mosquitoes.

ber 13.   Spent the day (after breakfast at the hotel) at Mr. Royle's, where I wrote letters home and lunched—again regally. Upon my word, I do not wonder that Mr. and Mrs. Royle are the friends of the great as well as the small. Their house is a palace, and their entertainment worthy of the royal owner of a royal abode. On the staircase are mummies of great ones who lived and died 300 years before the days of Christ, and whose many coloured outer cerements are as bright as when Egyptian artists followed Egyptian embalmers, and the two combined to show us the durability of ancient art. From the roof of their house—the finest in Port Said—you gaze out upon the busy Port, the entrance to the Canal, the waters of the Great Sea, and the sandy deserts of the Great Continent. I shall see, of course, places more thoroughly Eastern, but here I first saw the *yasmack*, the covering for the faces of the women; here the camel as a beast of burden; here that men wear petticoats and women trousers; here the water-carriers—men with goatskin bags slung across their backs, and women with bottles on their heads—and here the counterfeit presentment of many an Ali Baba. To me, therefore, Port Said will stand clearly out on the pages of life and memory. I left about 5 o'clock on board the Austrian Lloyd's steamship "Ceres," for Jaffa and the Holy Land. Everywhere and with everybody the name of Cook acted as an *open sesame*, and I received, in consequence, from the agent of Lloyd's, the landlord of the hotel, the turbanned boots, and the bare-legged porter, the utmost respect and attention. The "Ceres" is much smaller, of course, than the "Kaisar," but it is a nice vessel, the saloon mirrored and decorated in pleasant, homely style. Only three persons besides myself as passengers—two Americans and one Norwegian, bound, like myself, for the Holy Land. The night was very beautiful, with a nearly full moon, and I walked the raised deck or sat in its reclining seats alone until nearly 10 o'clock. Whilst there a turbanned Mussulman came up, spread his carpet, and went silently and solemnly through his lengthened prayers and genuflexions. I had never seen this before, though I had often read of it; and one's feelings were indescribable, journeying to the Holy Land, the land for ever hallowed by the footsteps of Christ, alone with this follower of a prophet who claimed a higher rank than the Christian's Saviour, his face towards Mecca, and his head bowed to the earth in adoration of the "one God, Allah, and Mahomet his prophet." Though our faiths are different, 1 yet felt we were one; we recognised a common Father, to be adored and worshipped, to be believed in and trusted.

From Jaffa to Jerusalem.

day, ber 14.

WE reached *Jaffa* at 9 o'clock. A clear, bright, and beautiful morning. The appearance of the town, built up from the rocky shore, and crowned with dome and minaret, was very striking. 'Tis often difficult to land here, but we were exceptionally favoured. More than a score of boats put off from the shore whence Jonah "found a ship going to Tarshish," and fled from the work though not the presence of his God. The rocks through which with strong stroke our boats were guided were the same upon which Jonah gazed. Even in his day it was a port of some importance. He paid his fare as we do now, and found a generous captain and a kindly though superstitious crew. Half a dozen dark-visaged Turks had boarded the vessel upon our casting anchor, having embroidered on their tunics "Cook's boatmen," and I afterwards learnt that even here Mr. C. has a large establishment, the entire staff numbering nearly a hundred. I am more than ever impressed with the greatness and the immense value of the gigantic undertakings of our good friend J. M. C. What shall I say of the place and of my feelings when I first trod the strand of the land for ever hallowed above all others? How true it is that words are too poor and language too weak to express our deepest feelings. It was another land and another people—novel and strange and delightful. We wended our way through narrow, ill-paved streets, brushing against countless scores of heavily-laden camels and asses, with their dirty but picturesque drivers and riders. The number of the people struck me with profound astonishment; they could be counted by the thousand. The hotel is just outside the town, close to groves of oranges and lemons, and sufficiently elevated to give us a view of the waters of the Mediterranean. Before breakfast, which was not to be had till 12 o'clock, I started out with my dragoman to see the town, and to call upon Miss Walker Arnott, to whom Mr. Cook had given me an introduction. My way was through the market-place, held in a very extensive unpaved square with rough caravansaries and sheds around, and with a motley body of folk buying and selling, haggling and quarrelling. Such strange wares : long green sugar-canes, nameless and unknown vegetables, radishes as large as carrots, green and brown dates, flat brown-baked cakes, salt fish like herrings, live chickens tied together by their legs, and cackling and struggling as they were held up to the possible buyer. The sellers pitched their goods where they liked, and it was no easy matter to work our way through the crouching Moslems, their goods, their camels, and their asses. Miss Arnott's Tabeetha Mission buildings are outside the city, as is our hotel—(the name of our hotel, by the way, is "The Jerusalem"). 'Tis a square, substantial building, with large entrance hall and lofty rooms for the girls, who number at the present time about fifty. The dormitories are large and well ventilated, and everything is neat and clean, and the children—girls—so happy looking ; it was a most agreeable change from the dirt and squalor outside. Miss Arnott has carried on the work for many years, and the erection of the new building was largely owing to the kindness and pecuniary help of Mr. Thomas Cook and his family. A cornerstone of the outer wall was taken from the supposed house of "Simon the Tanner," where Peter lodged ; and upon it, Miss Arnott told me, Mr. J. M. Cook had made a wise little speech on the occasion of the commencement of the building. I was introduced to a dear, bright little girl, who is one of Mr. Cook's *protegés*, and who bowed her head and kissed my hand so gracefully when we parted. I talked to the dear children for a few minutes about our common God, and heard them sing in Arabic and English some songs and hymns known to us all. Miss Arnott has devoted her life and her means to this work. She has Jewesses, Moslems, Copts, Catholics, and Protestants among her children. They are taught Arabic and English, and, where no objection is raised, are instructed in the Christian religion. Miss Arnott has a worn, but a sweet face ; she has recently lost her sister, and has had many trials and troubles during her long residence here. In the afternoon I attended the English church, an irregular-shaped, unpretentious building near Miss Arnott's school. The walls are whitewashed, and the floors paved with common tiles. The people were of a different colour and race to myself, but the service of our English church, and, above all, the well-known hymns, "Come let us join our cheerful songs," "I came to Jesus," and "Just as I am," with English texts issued by English societies, and a small harmonium, with the well-known names of Silber and Fleming upon it, made one quite at home, and to feel gratefully how wide-reaching is English civilisation and English benevolence. We received inestimable blessings from the East, and we are endeavouring by wise missionary effort to repay some of the debt we owe. The sermon was preached from John iv. 4 ; the place made it interesting, but otherwise it was in no way remarkable. After this I was taken by my dragoman into the finest of the many orange groves of Jaffa ; picked the large oval-shaped oranges from the trees, ate my fill, and brought away a pocketful, with the full concurrence of the turbanned gardener, who seemed very grateful for the franc I gave him. The irrigation is very complete, and the channels round the trees are filled twice a day with water raised by water-wheels, and passed down roughly-made conduits that intersect the groves. From here I was taken to the flat roof of a building recently erected by some rich Copts at Cairo for their poorer brethren here. I can give but a faint notion of the deeply interesting scene. Looking over the town, with its square buildings, its lofty minarets, and here and there its rounded roofs which indicated school or temple, was the gloriously blue Mediterranean—"the great sea" of our Saviour's time. Turning round and looking eastward, were orange groves of vast extent ; and beyond, the *Plains of Sharon*, with their promise of blossom, flower, and fruit. Still further on were the *Mountains of Judæa*, that looked down on their further slopes upon Zion, the city of the Great King—Jerusalem the Golden. To the right, looking south, was the road to Gaza and Philistia, while away to the north was the desert stretching away to the Carmel range of mountains, and the not far distant land of the Samaritans. 'Twas a heavenly day, and with emotions too strong for expression, I slowly descended from my veritable mount of vision, like to that whence Moses saw the promised land to which he had brought his people, but into which he was never to enter. My hotel is pleasantly situated: from its gardens I look out upon orange groves and the distant city, built up the sides of a small acclivity immediately overlooking the sea. I can see the blue waters of the Mediterranean, hear the hum of insect life, and rejoice that all is as peaceful as a Sabbath-day should be. The tall and feathery palms, with their hanging clusters of ripening dates, rise here and there in the midst of oranges and lemons and around me are the cactus, palm, and other trees of Eastern origin and growth, all strange as a waking dream. Unfortunately I had not time to visit the reputed house of Simon the Tanner, where Peter lodged. It overlooks the sea, and may be the *site* of that interesting abode. The frequent sieges to which Jaffa has been exposed would render it impossible that it should be the house itself. Few towns have been so often overthrown, sacked, pillaged, burned, and rebuilt. I looked with awed and indignant interest at the hospital in which Napoleon the First had 500 of his own wounded soldiers poisoned, on the plea that he thereby saved them from Mussulman barbarities; and upon the Strand where he shot in cold blood 4,000 Albanians who had delivered up their arms upon the promise of quarter. 'Tis an old view of mine, and Jaffa increases my belief of its truth, that Napoleon was the nearest approach in the family of man to the apocalyptic Anti-christ, and fulfilled in himself all that is supposed to distinguish that embodiment of evil.

November 15. Started at 5 o'clock for *Jerusalem*. Although only forty miles distant, yet, through the wretched roads, 'tis a long day's journey. My carriage (one of Cook and Son's) is well built, with springs of steel, much like a French diligence, with hood in front, and room for four and luggage in the body of it. The three small mustang-looking horses, harnessed abreast, were driven by a bright-looking young Turk with baggy trousers and long blue coat and fez. We started in the dark, my dragoman mounted by the side of the driver. We drove through the town and among sleeping camels, with their dirty Arab masters resting between them. On the outskirts I saw a dead camel drawn up by the side of the roadway under the cactus hedge, and, strange to say, later in the day, when going over the mountains of Judæa, I saw also a dead donkey! Our road was through miles of orange groves, with lofty hedges of the prickly pear, which stood out very weird-like in the starlit morning. As morning broke, we reached the Jaffa side of the plains of Sharon, and I saw them bathed in golden brilliancy by the sun rising over the Judæan hills. The road was atrocious and the jolting intolerable, yet the day will be ever memorable and ever delightful. How could it be otherwise ? We came out into the road that Peter had often travelled. We passed the traditional site of the raising of Tabitha—*Lydda*. We drove through *Ramleh* with its lofty Tower—the Arimathea of the rich man whose sepulchre received the body of Christ; skirted *Gaza*, passed into *Philistia*, saw *Emmaus*, where Jesus met His sorrowing, doubting followers after His resurrection ; and *Mizpeh*, picturesquely placed on one of the mountains whence Samuel offered sacrifice and Saul was crowned, and where Joshua obtained his great victory over the five kings led by Adoni-zedec, King of Jerusalem ; passed by the side of the valley of *Ajalon*, ascended the mountains to *Kirjath-Jearim*, entered the land belonging to the tribe of Benjamin, saw the supposed site of Obed Edom's house, where the Ark of God abode for three months, and whence David bore it with dancing and with trumpets and shawms, and so sadly shocked his wife Michal ; saw, nestled under the hills, the birthplace of John the Baptist ; gazed out along the valley where David slew Goliath with a

sling and a stone ; and finally—alighting from the carriage, for
none can enter the narrow streets—entered Jerusalem by the
Jaffa Gate, with the Tower of David frowning down upon us,
square and solid, a worthy place to be the traditional Tower of
the King ! Despite the tiring journey, the burning sun, the
jolting over roads like the rocky bed of dried-up mountain
torrents, it was one long day of delight. We saw camels and
asses innumerable ; large flocks of black, long-eared, short-tailed
goats ; cows and bullocks, small as the Kerry breed ; plenty of
little birds like the fieldfare, but with crested head ; here and
there an eagle of the smaller sort ; plenty of lizards, larger
and uglier than those of Botzen ; olive trees, and the peasants
gathering in their olive harvest ; husbandmen ploughing with
the same sort of plough as did the men of Christ's day, so slight
that a boy could carry it, and so useless that as it scraped the
soil the rank grass remained, and tares could grow even before
the good seed was sown. We lunched half-way in a mosque-like
building by the wayside, in which the pigeons roosted and the
hens pecked and cackled, and laid their eggs and brought up
their families, none molesting, none making them afraid.

IN JERUSALEM.

November 16. OUR hotel is a characteristic building and most interestingly situated. The hotel at Jaffa, looking out upon the Mediterranean, was called the "Jerusalem Hotel," and this, looking out upon Jerusalem, is called the "Mediterranean Hotel"; so if wrong be done at Jaffa, the wrong is righted at Jerusalem. The building consists of three floors, all of stone—stone walls, more than four feet thick, stone floors, stone roof; the ceiling, or rather roof of each floor, is groined like the crypt of a cathedral ; the staircases, of course of stone, run up in an open courtyard, and you enter dining-room and bedroom from a square open to the sky; the bedroom walls are whitewashed and the dining-room rudely painted. The place is clean. Mats are placed in your bedroom and in the dining-room; and the pigeons—let us say doves—nestle and coo at your windows. The mosquitoes are not quite so bad as at Port Said, but they are bad enough, and I suffer terribly from their bites. You don't see them, but you hear them, and, above all, you *feel* them. You don't know whence they come, but you undoubtedly know *where* they go: a small red pimple, followed by intolerable itching, leave you in no doubt about *that*. Mr. and Mrs. Lawson are here: he is the youngest member of the House of Commons, is the son of the proprietor of the *Daily Telegraph*, and the nephew of my friends, Mr. and Mrs. George Phillips (Sir Benjamin Phillips' son). He is not unlike Lord Rosebery, both as to his youthful looks, his height, his regular features, and his pleasant smile. We had plenty of talk together. He is very clever, has already made his mark, and is one of the men of the future; but I find that he, like so many others, has very strange notions about the City, and knows very little either of its constitution or its work.

If I see nothing more, I am more than satisfied and delighted by the view from the roof of my hotel, which is flat, and rises above the nearer houses. As the site is that of Zion's holy hill, and is elevated and close to the Jaffa Gate, I can see almost round the city, and nearly everything that makes Jerusalem so memorable. Away before me, so close that I can almost count its trees, is the *Mount of Olives*, crowned by a French and Russian church, with a small mosque between. Below is *Gethsemane*, sacred to the Saviour's sorrows; and below that the bed of the *Kedron*, no longer a running brook. Nearer to me, and shutting out the Valley of Jehoshaphat, is the Mosque of Omar, upon Mount Moriah, on the site of the Temple of David, in a splendid state of preservation. Domes and minarets on the right and left of me, and, immediately below my windows, the *Pool of Hezekiah*, a great receptacle for rainwater, surrounded by buildings, where the people draw, by rope and windlass, their supplies of water in strange-looking leathern buckets. A little to the left of me is the church of the Holy Sepulchre, built by Helena, the mother of Constantine the Great, who gave name to Constantinople. In the distance, but more to the right, are the Mountains of Moab. On the other side is the Tower of King David, whence tradition says —not more truthful here than elsewhere—David first saw the wife of Uriah. Close by is the Jaffa Gate, one of five (there once were twelve) which give entrance to the city. Directly round, to the left, is the road to Bethlehem ; and below, the Valley of Hinnom, where the people of Israel, in the day of their degradation, offered their children to Moloch. All around stretch the walls of the city. Immediately facing the entrance to the hotel is David's street, forming part of Mount Zion, and leading to the Tomb of the King. Far away on the left, on the hill-top, is Nob, where David, being hungered, ate of the shewbread without sin, Abimelech consenting. How much more delightful and interesting to me, ever after this, will be the Scriptures of the Old Testament ! No doubt much that will be shown me will be altogether fanciful and untrue, but the city stands where the city of David stood; the hills are the same that looked down about Jerusalem in the days of our Lord ; the land is the same ; and the moon, the sun, and the stars. I could scarcely tear myself away from the view to attend to the necessary wants of life. After breakfast my dragoman came to take me to some of the nearer places of interest. We first visited the Church of St. James. Here is supposed to have been the scene of his martyrdom. A stone is shown where he was beheaded, as well as the tomb of the saint, over which an Arminian Convent is erected. Afterwards we went to the House of the High Priest, and saw the Hall in which Christ was examined by Caiaphas, and denied by Peter ; the stone to which He was tied to be scourged is shown, and a niche in the church, said to have been His narrow prison. As the place where ancient traditions gather all that is identified with the sufferings of Christ, we cannot look at the building and its surroundings without interest, though the feeling is not accompanied with faith. This latter building is outside the city walls. We have passed through King David's Gate, and now wend our way through a Jewish churchyard to the Tomb of the Great King. This is a very ancient building, and there is little reason to doubt that here David and Solomon were buried, and that near here was David's Palace and Solomon's, and the scene of the greatness and grandeur of which our Bibles tell. Thence we went to one of the best of the modern institutions of the place—Bishop Gobat's English School. He was the second Bishop of Jerusalem, and lies in the adjoining churchyard with his wife and some of his children. Mr. Palmer, the teacher, took me over the schools, and showed me the progress of the scholars, who are chiefly the children of Christian converts from Mahommedanism and Judaism. Opposite the schools, which are literally hewn out of the great rock upon which David's palace stood, across the intervening valley, are the low-lying houses, with somewhat extensive grounds, built by the late philanthropist, Sir Moses Montefiore, for the poor Jews of Jerusalem. The Vale of Hinnom adjoins the place. As we returned, just before we reached the Jaffa Gate, we saw huddled together a number of lepers—miserable, forlorn wretches—appealing in their misery to the charity of the passer-by. After lunch we went through some of the narrow business streets—alleys, rather—of Jerusalem. The squalor and dirt of the people and their surroundings are very noticeable. Dust and dirt and flies and dogs; infinite variety in dress; every possible gradation of colour, from faces fair as albinos to those dark as negroes. Here some of the fairest-skinned men are Jews—Spanish Jews, I am told. We went over the remains of the vast buildings left by the Knights of St. John, the old Crusaders of Richard's days; the land and buildings were given recently to the Emperor of Germany by the Sultan, and, at the expense of the German Government, a large part has been cleared, and the church and cloisters, the vast wells, aqueducts and buildings for the knights, have been exposed. A small German church is built on a part of the ruins, and doubtless by-and-by the work will be continued and the whole site cleared. We passed on to the *Via Doloroso*, down which our Saviour is said to have borne His cross. Here and there stones—of course apocryphal—are marked out as those against which the Man of Sorrows leant with His heavy burden; many superstitious Christians—Greek and Roman Catholic—make pilgrimages to the spot, and have worn away the stones with their devout kisses. I went into a deeply interesting convent and church, that of the Sisters of Zion, which have been built upon part of Pilate's house. A very ancient arch is shown where Pilate sat to judge the Man in whom no fault was found. One of the sisters showed me the schools, in which some 150 children are taught, and many of them clothed and boarded, and a part of the pavement of the real Via Doloroso in the time of the Saviour, which goes some twelve or fifteen feet under the present roadway. We passed through the Damascus Gate, older and far finer than that of Jaffa, round the walls where very extensive explorations are proceeding, and so to my hotel. I called, with Mr. Cook's introduction, upon Mr. Bergheim : he is the banker of the place, and his sons are clever, intelligent men of business, with engineering tastes. They took me to see the mill they are erecting for the grinding of corn. They are about to put up an "Otto" gas engine of 12-horse power, and hope to work it with petroleum. Some idea may be formed of the fierce character of the Mussulman population here by what has occurred to Mr. Bergheim's eldest son. An estate was bought by him some time since, which interfered with the supposed rights of some Mussulman squatters (for the Land question is a trouble elsewhere than in Ireland), and a few months ago the poor young fellow, the father of five dear little children, was murdered on his way from Jaffa, his own servant being one of the murderers; none have been convicted, although there is little doubt as to those who are guilty. Sir Edward Lechmere, the member for Worcester-

shire, is here ; so we have two members of Parliament and one
who tried to be. Not bad for an hotel in Jerusalem, in the
month of November! Lady Lechmere is an active member of
the Greek Church.

FROM JERUSALEM TO JERICHO.

17. STARTED early for our great visit to *Jordan, Jericho*, and the
Dead Sea. Our cavalcade was numerous and very imposing ; I wish it were in my power to describe it fully and
accurately. An American gentleman and his wife—Mr. and Mrs.
Chandler—accompanied me, and this added, of course, to our
number and our importance. There were first two armed
Bedouin chiefs or sheiks, who are paid by the Government, and
who are responsible for our safety. They rode Arab horses, had
long muskets slung across their backs, revolvers in their belts,
and dirks and scimitars at their sides ; they were dressed very
picturesquely, and their horses were richly caparisoned ; then
came myself and Mr. and Mrs. C., our two dragomen, a Turkish
cook (for nothing is to be had by the way save what we ourselves
prepare), a Greek carrying our baggage on a sumpter-mule, and
another with our provisions for three days—in all ten persons.
We were upon Syrian horses, smaller than ours at home ; all save
us Europeans were attired in Eastern dress, and all armed. The
wandering Bedouins are robbers by profession, and are very fierce
and numerous. It really was a very pretty sight, not the less
so that a graceful-looking lady was of the party, dressed in an
ordinary riding habit, but with a far-reaching hat to protect her
from the sun. We skirted the northern walls of Jerusalem,
past the Damascus Gate, through the Mahommedan and Jewish
burial-ground, past the Beautiful Gate of the ancient Temple,
along the side of Kedron, through the Valley of Jehoshaphat,
past the tomb of the Virgin, and very close to the Garden of

Gethsemane and the Mount of Olives. The place where Stephen was stoned was pointed out to us : a very likely spot, a part of the ancient rock, not far from one of the Gates of Jerusalem named after the Martyr. Before long we reached *Bethany*, where Lazarus, Martha, and Mary lived ; where our Lord spent His few happy days, where He raised Lazarus from the dead, and not far from whence He ascended after His resurrection. The place, like so many that are notable, is built on the side of a hill, and in the days of Israel's greatness was, no doubt, a pretty village, where wealthy Jews would resort; but now it is a place of dens and hovels, inhabited by a wretched population of Arab peasants. Further on, to the right of our road, we passed *Bethphage*, where the Lord sent His disciples for the ass upon which He was to make His triumphant entry into Jerusalem and the Temple. By the way, although the poor little donkeys so cruelly laden by their task-masters are generally of the most ordinary kind, we see some very splendid fellows, fit for Eastern pageantry, and not unworthy to bear kings and princes on their way. We had now fairly entered the *Wilderness* in which John the Baptist preached the need of repentance, and to which came the inhabitants of Jerusalem and all the regions round about. I saw many an ascetic-looking, gaunt and cadaverous man, as John must have been, clothed in camel's-hair and goatskin, and with leathern girdle about his loins. Nothing is more striking than the permanence of Bible pictures, of men and manners in the far-off ages, and the reproduction to-day of every salient feature. Bare rocks and hills, mountains without verdure and valleys without water, hot and dusty was our way, as it had been in the time when Jesus trod the earth—aye, and long ages before. We stopped for lunch at a roughly-enclosed yard with covered entrance—the inn of the Good Samaritan—on the top of the Mountains of Judæa, from whence we could see the waters of the Dead Sea. A miserable-looking man, shoeless, as so many are, and clothed in a long blue gaberdine, with sash and fez, is in charge, and receives a trifle (about a penny) from every traveller who rests beneath the shade of this khan in the Desert. Our lunch was a good one, and we had water from the Apostle's well, a fountain passed by us, not far from Bethphage. The heat had been almost intolerable, and we were glad to stay an hour and a half here before recommencing our journey. We came in sight of the Valley of the Jordan and the blue waters of the Dead Sea about three o'clock, but it was nearly five before we reached our abode for the night—a prettily-built light wooden structure, with overhanging trellis-work, through which the vine trailed very gracefully. The place was built by a Russian lady, and is furnished plainly, but with all things essential—all clean and sweet. No provisions can be had there, but our cook and our dragoman had brought everything needful, and we had a dinner not surpassed by any I have had since leaving the "Kaisar." Soup, fish, entrées, sweets, fruits, coffee, tea—and oh, such tea! some for which Messrs. Cook and Sons are responsible, I dare swear—everything we could wish for. *Jericho*, as a place of habitation, has long since ceased to be, although the ruins of two ancient Jerichos are pointed out to us : the one which Joshua went round about, and which fell at the seven times repeated blowing of the trumpets ; another, built by Herod, when he came here for bathing in the day of his power; and modern Jericho, the place in which we find ourselves—just a green oasis in the Desert. The waters from the Pool of Elisha are cleverly used for irrigating a strip of this desert plain, and verily it is covered with verdure, and blossoms like the rose ! The thorn (the *dona*), with which the Saviour's piercing crown was made, grows in great abundance ; it makes the only fencing, hedge and firing for the people. In the walled enclosures are the oleander, with its beautiful but poisonous flowers, the plantain or banana tree, oranges, citrons and lemons, olives, trailing vines, figs, the pomegranate, and vegetables of various kinds, all growing fairly luxuriantly. But 'tis a tiny spot in the Great Desert, and extends no further than where the waters from the Pool are brought. The only thing I have seen done by the Turkish

Government for the people is what is done here to utilise the
waters of the fountain that Elisha is supposed to have
miraculously healed. A very handsome stone aqueduct
is carried over the bed of the Brook Cherith (where
Isaiah was fed by the ravens), and brings the waters into
the village at a height sufficient to enable the inhabitants
to fill their trenches with the vitalising fluid.* We sit under
the open verandah while our dinners are being prepared, the
trailing vine floating in the cool evening air, and innumerable
insect life, hornets in great force, making all things vocal.
When our dinner was ended our guides and servants had their
repast, and with them one or two of their friends; one was a
handsome young Arab of about six-and-twenty, about whom
my dragoman told me a tale of blood and revenge. Twenty
years ago, when the man was a child of five or six, his father
and uncle were killed by the chief of a neighbouring tribe of
Bedouins—a man of notoriously bloodthirsty character—and his
mother taken by force to become the murderer's wife. The child
was away at the time at an uncle's in the Jordan valley. Ten
years after, when the boy was sixteen, the murderer of his
father was pointed out to him in the wilderness we have just
passed; the boy attacked the man, shot him dead, cut off his
head, and took the bleeding trophy of his vengeance to his
mother, who had lived a wretched life with the man who had
stolen her in her youth. This deed was so much a matter of
course that no inquiry followed. The twice tragically-widowed
wife went cheerfully to the tent of her son, and the young lad
became the hero of his tribe; whilst an uncle gave him his
daughter to wife, without payment (for here, by the way, the
dower comes from the husband, not, as with us, with the wife).
The man was dark and handsome, dressed as all the Bedouins
are, but with a little more ornament upon his rifle than is usual,
and with a longer scimitar than any I had before seen. The

---

* I must withdraw even this, for I learn that the valley is the Sultan's
private possession, and that the works have been done for himself, and to
improve his own property.

place abounds with game : partridges, quails, gazelles, wild boars, tigers (occasionally), leopards, jackals, foxes, &c. At night the jackals came round the enclosure, and kept up their short, sharp bark far into the night. My two travelling companions are American, very agreeable and intelligent; and although Mr. Chandler indulges a good deal in "yes, sir" and "I guess," he is not half a bad fellow. He is tall, dark, and well shaped, with a Roman nose and a rather severe look; he is taciturn, and is very proud of his wife, who is eight years his junior, but looks still younger. She is fair and slim, with splendid brown hair; was a graduate at one of the oldest of the American universities, paints and sings, has written a book (a copy of which she has promised to send me), rides well, and is generally an interesting person, though I should think not likely to make "old bones." They have one child, who is—his parents being my authority—a very clever lad : he can play the violin, paint, ride the bicycle and the horse equally well, can make steam engines, has invented an improvement on the lines of sailing ships, and is just 13! There is a wonderful deal of simplicity about them. They both believe in the Bible implicitly, literally, and totally. The Scriptures referring to the scenes of the day are read by him, while she, as the reading goes on, exclaims, "Just think, now !" "How delightful !" "Well, now !" "Wasn't it good of Him ?" &c., as though she had heard these things for the first time, had never read the Bible, and felt it necessary to express her approval right away. It was very wicked of me, but her simplicity reminded me of the tale of the sailor, who, being unused to church and the horrified listener to a sermon upon the death of Christ, attacked and nearly murdered a poor Jew whom he met at the church door; and when remonstrated with by his victim and told that a tale so old in no way justified his conduct, excused himself by the plea that he had only just heard that the Jews were the murderers of his Master ! The way in which her husband talks of her water-colours, and of her talents, accomplishments, and good looks, must be a little trying to his wife, and tests her modesty and her blushes ; she only says, however, " Now, George, dear, I can't help looking young." " 'Tis good, dear, but you think too much of these things ; if you said that of Georgy," &c., by which I understand that she is a sensible sort of woman, but rather likes the flattery, and thinks she really is clever and pretty and young.

November 18.   A perfect contrast to yesterday, but equally tiring. That was a scene of rocky mountains and stony defiles, ascending high among mountains or low 'mid the wadys. To-day a bare sandy plain, a very land as well as sea of death. We were a fairly imposing party, but our attendants were not so numerous as before : one, instead of two armed Bedouins, two dragomen, and one attendant with our lessened baggage, with water-bags hanging at his saddle's side, and with provisions for the way. We passed through a Moslem burial-place, just outside modern Jericho, which, like most others we have seen, is unenclosed, and consists of small squares of rough stones, with here and there an attempt at a fixed memorial. Round one some women and children were wailing over their dead—a sad and solemn sight in the early morning. Passing very quickly through the ancient *Gilgal*,—now the abode of wandering Arabs, having the worst of characters, "thieves to a man," says our dragoman, burrowing like rabbits in heaps of earth, covered cairns rather than houses, dirty and wretched, more so even than are the homes of the present inhabitants of Bethany,—we entered upon the Desert, and for nearly three hours jogged over the waste plains of the Dead Sea, passing, far up in the Judæan mountains, the place assigned by Mahommedan tradition—despite the Bible account—as the burying-place of Moses, over which a mosque and convent have been erected. Sand and earth, mixed with powdered chalk and sandstone, formed our trackless way, with a few stunted herb-like shrubs dotted here and there. About 10.30 we reached the northern edge of the Sea that marks the site of Sodom and Gomorrah. We had been travelling nearly three

The Dead Sea.

hours to a place that looked within rifle-shot of our bedroom windows. Here Mr. Chandler and I bathed. Never shall we forget our sensations. The sea is clear and blue, and so buoyant that floating is easy and sinking impossible: the water is salt and bitter as the waters of Marah. I need not add that there is no truth in the many sensational tales about this notable inland sea. Birds fly over its waters in safety. No noisome exhalations proceed from its banks or render barren its borders. From thence we turned in a north-easterly direction for Jordan, which empties itself into the sea it never fills, close under the low range of the Mountains of Moab. The plain of the Jordan differs but slightly from the plain of the Dead Sea, of which, indeed, it forms a part; but as we approached the stream we saw the line of willowy trees that mark the course of the sacred river. Just before we reached our resting-place we were shown the spot, approached by sloping sides, where the Saviour was baptised by John, and the Sacred Dove descended in token of the divinity of Him who desired "to fulfil all righteousness." Our camping-ground was at the edge of the ford over which the Israelites are supposed to have passed before the siege and capture of Jericho; it was enclosed in waving trees of the tamarisk order, and there was pleasant shelter for our midday repast. A mounted Bedouin forded the stream, which was scarcely above his saddlegirths, while an armed and mounted sheikh stood silhouetted upon the sky-line on the opposite cliff, which rose sheer up upon the other side of Jordan. Three savage-looking Bedouins were bathing at the ford; and afterwards we had some half-dozen women, with long blue skirts and black braided hair, to sing to us—if the strange monotonous chant, accompanied by the beating of their hands, could be called singing. We gave them backsheesh, which was divided among them by our dragoman. They have a very stately walk, with tattooed faces, dark eyes, and an expression by no means unpleasing, but dirty beyond telling. After two hours' rest we filled our water bottles with Jordan water, remounted our horses—not before, however, Mrs. Chandler had taken a very striking sketch of the ford and its surroundings—and started across the plain for our pleasant resting-place. We could see before us the long line of the Mountains of Judæa ; in the far distance, between an opening in the hills, the top of the tower surmounting the Mount of Olives ; away to the front the modern town of Jericho—of which our hotel, a small Greek church, and a Russian house for pilgrims, are the chief buildings ; the dirty hovels that mark what was once a city of some renown, *Gilgal;* the Mountain of Temptation, whence tradition says the Saviour was shown "all the kingdoms of the world and the glory of them." Behind us were the Mountains of Moab, Pisgah, the holy place whence Moses saw the long-promised land into which he should never enter ; and away up the valley, to the north, just a glimpse of Hermon —all very delightful, all very impressive. As we neared home a long caravan of asses and camels passed us, laden with corn for the Jerusalem market, the bells of the camels jingling faintly upon the desert air. As we entered the walled enclosure of our house we heard the monotonous sound of the tomtom, as some dervishes passed on their way to Jerusalem. We were told by our dragoman that the bare valley of the Jordan through which we had passed is grass-grown in the spring and early summer, and that here the Bedouins bring the camels and their young to feed upon the succulent grasses. Our evening finished most suitably. Some dozen dark-looking, characteristically-dressed Bedouins of Jericho came in to shout their fierce war-songs, led by their chief, who commenced the song facing them, not the audience. They were gathered under the outer vine-covered verandah, and hanging lamps shining upon their dark bearded faces, made the scene wild and fierce beyond telling. Especially was this the case when their leader took the long scimitar of our Bedouin guard from its scabbard, and whirled it round his head, with shouts, to which his followers responded with fierce gestures and much clapping of hands. Tired from the excitement of the day,

The Ford of the Jordan.

we all went to our beds before 9 o'clock, though it was
long before the barking of the dogs and sharp cries of the
jackals enabled me to sleep.

RETURN TO JERUSALEM.

19. WE started about 7 o'clock on our return to Jerusalem. Our
cavalcade was constituted as on Wednesday, the cook and
his henchman bringing up the rear. There never was so
good or so good-tempered a cook the wide world over. He cannot
speak a word of English, but is constantly jabbering to us,
and constantly laughing, and keeps us all in capital humour.
We laugh at him, the rest laugh with him, and he is perfectly
safe for backsheesh when his labours are ended. We traced the
bright little stream from Elisha's Pool to its source—a hole in
the mountain, and reminded ourselves that the Bible said it
should last FOR EVER, and that we had before us the evidence
of the truth of these writings of thousands of years ago. After
picking our way among the remains of Joshua's Jericho, we
struck across to our mountain road, and shortly commenced
the toilsome ascent. On our way we passed the cairn which
showed where the headless trunk of the assassin lies whose
executioner we saw two nights ago. There are many such cairns
in the Jordan Valley, for there the fiercest of the Bedouins
live. We lunched at the Apostle's Pool, a rough place, where a
cool spring bursts out of the earth, and where a few thorn trees
gave us some trifling shelter from the heat of the sun. Here
we saw another Bible statement verified : the goatherd calling
his flock from the hills for watering : "they know his voice and
follow him"—no dog, the shepherd only. We saw in the distance
David's Cave of Adullam, and returning on the other side of
the Mount of Olives, dismounted and walked through the
Garden of Gethsemane. The space occupied by this deeply-

interesting garden is only about one-third of an acre; it is surrounded by a stucco-covered wall, and is under the control of the Franciscans, one of whom admitted us to the sacred enclosure. In it are eight olive trees, so gnarled and twisted, so large and venerable, not unlikely to be the veritable trees growing in the Saviour's time. Some olive trees were pointed out to me in the gardens of the young Bergheims, believed to be more than a hundred years old, that were very small, and that had not, I was assured, appreciably increased in the twenty or thirty years during which they had belonged to the family. A few flowers are grown in the well-watered enclosure, and a few rude frescoes represent scenes in the life of Christ. The place of the Saviour's agony is pointed out, a rocky place where the disciples slept, and the spot where the kiss of Judas was given. Very many look upon this as the actual scene of the agony and betrayal, and with such thoughts and beliefs one echoes the words of the Mosaic record—"Take off thy shoes from off thy feet, for the place whereon thou standest is holy ground." My dragoman arranged to have our group photographed: with what success I have yet to learn. The parable of the difficulties of rich men and the needle's eye of the Saviour's warning was illustrated very forcibly on our return through the Jaffa Gate. A string of horses, asses, and camels was coming out of the city as we entered, when one of the camels attempted and failed to pass through the narrow gate, which is called the Needle's Eye; and we saw at once, though for a camel it might be possible, yet if loaded the passage would be impracticable.

November 20. Slept fairly well, despite the mosquitoes. Took my morning look from the housetop over Jerusalem; very delightful. Read again the account of the Crucifixion. One may be pardoned for feeling some doubt whether the Church of the Holy Sepulchre is the true scene of the trial, judgment, execution, and burial of Christ. Still, I look around me, and feel on holy ground. The life of the Day of the Lord continues still, and one sees again the fickle multitude who received Him as the Promised One, and ere long cried, "Crucify Him! Crucify

Robinson's Arch.

Him!" The day devoted to Jerusalem and its traditional sites. Three days in the saddle finds me very stiff, and with little wonder, considering the nature of the roads. My dragoman, was here at 9 o'clock to take me to some of the most notable of the city sights, but quite a different dragoman from that of the day before. Dressed and mounted for our Jericho trip, he was booted, spurred, caparisoned in baggy trousers, embroidered jacket, Bedouin headdress, with coil of camel's hair, and with pistol and yatagan at his side. This morning, though the dark Arab face was the same, the dress was more peaceful and less picturesque—a short jacket, long petticoat, stockingless legs, and fez only. Our first visit was to the Wailing-place of the Jews, a very ancient wall at the back of the Mosque of Omar, a part, there is little if any doubt, of the second Temple. There were some sixty Jews and Jewesses—the sexes choosing different parts of the wall—reading from their Scriptures, and chanting their low, wailing petitions, rocking the body, and moving the head in unison. They were all cleanly dressed in their Sabbath best, and were of all ages—some noble faces among them. Deeply impressed with the scene and its surroundings. We passed on to the Arch discovered by Robinson, after whom it was named, which marks the commencement of the viaduct connecting Mount Moriah with Mount Zion, over the Terapean Valley. From thence to the Dung Gate, the smallest of the gates of the city, but little used, up to the top of the walls under the Hill of Zion. Here there was a magnificent view of what cannot have changed since the days of Christ. The town of Siloam, and the pool in which the blind man was directed to wash; the gardens of Solomon, the place where Absolom killed his brother Ammon, his tomb; the Hill of Evil Counsel, and the Field of Blood where Judas hanged himself; the Valley of Jehoshaphat; on the right the Mount of Olives, and on the left the Mountains of Moab, misty and blue in the dim distance. We went through the Jews' quarter to the chief of their synagogues. The whole place reeked with vegetable garbage and Eastern filth. The

Arabs and Mahomedans are dirty, the Jews filthy beyond the powers of description. Thence we went to the British Ophthalmic Hospital. On our road my dragoman stopped the first of a long string of camels, led by an Arab lad in the usual rough sheepskin coat, small turban, and with bare legs, and I had my first ride upon this interesting beast. As he knelt down he grunted and groaned in a way perfectly alarming to a novice. The movement of the body of the camel is altogether different from that of the horse : one side appears to advance, leaving the other lagging behind ; and as one's own anatomy is not prepared for this, the sensation is singular, and if a long journey be attempted must be found very disagreeable. The dismounting was an undertaking, but was successfully accomplished, and some trifling backsheesh rewarded the compliant driver. The resident head of the Hospital is Dr. Ogilvie, a young Scotchman, clever, devoted to this special work, and recognised as an authority in all matters surgical. I was most hospitably received, and was shown over the hospital, where as many as 1,200 patients in a month are successfully treated. I lunched with the Doctor and Mrs. Ogilvie, and afterwards went with them a few miles on the road to Bethlehem, where we had tea in the olive groves of the Greek Convent, and met Mr. Moore, the British Consul, and his family—very cultured and charming people. An exceedingly pleasant afternoon. There were some evidences of class differences and jealousies even in this little community of Europeans, but with all this, life in Jerusalem is clearly not so disagreeable as one might imagine. I heard on my return that a Jew of Jerusalem, on his way to Jaffa with money and securities of great value, had been robbed and murdered by Bedouins, and his body frightfully disfigured. The painful thing is that these crimes are done almost with impunity, and, in the case of a Jew, scarcely even the form of an inquiry is instituted. Life is very unsafe, and has become more so since executions have been discontinued. A few months' imprisonment, even where the guilt is brought home, with a liberal use of backsheesh on the part of the criminal, and he is again at large. The punishment of offenders and the administration of justice are altogether questions of money.

<small>Sunday, ovember 21.</small> To the Church of the Holy Sepulchre. This was my first exhaustive visit to this deeply interesting building. Under its ample dome all the chief events of the crucifixion and burial are supposed to have taken place. You are shown the place where Christ was nailed to the cross ; the place of crucifixion ; the stone where His body was laid when taken from the cross ; the spot where the soldiers plaited the crown of thorns and divided His garments ; the grave hewn out of the rock where His body was laid and the stone rolled against the entrance thereof ; the place where Helena discovered the CROSS upon which the Saviour suffered, and the tomb of Joseph of Arimathea. All this demands a good deal of faith on the part of the visitor ; but there are not wanting good men, thoughtful and intelligent, who believe it all absolutely ; for myself, I am content to know that somewhere near here the grave tragedy was completed that ended the life of the Man of Sorrows. All the various Churches of the Christians of the East are found within the walls of the building, which must have been very magnificent when fresh from the builders' hands, and still bears evidence of splendour, external and internal : the Greeks, the Latins, the Copts, the Armenians, the Syrians, and the Abyssinians have each their Church, but none are of any moment save the Greek : this occupies the centre of the building, and is magnificently adorned, and abounds in the votive offerings of the faithful. When we were there the Greek patriarch—a fine old man—was dispensing, from a magnificent chair, morsels of bread to the people who passed him in endless numbers. The crowd was too great for me to follow to see whether the wine was also given. None but Christians are admitted, but it is a painful fact that some eight or ten Mussulmans are seated on mats in a recess at the entrance to keep order, should the unseemly disturbances that more than once have been occur again. No Jew dare come even into the immediate

approaches to the building ; death would be the penalty. After this I went to the English church, and heard an excellent sermon from the resident Protestant clergyman, Mr. Kirk. The church is cruciform, and is somewhat handsomely built, of course in stone. I was struck with the number of children, Arab and Jewish converts, as well as those of Christian parents, that filled the place. I learn that in Jerusalem and the surrounding districts the number of Christians of all sects exceeds the Jews, as they again exceed the Moslem population in number. Lunched with Mr. and Mrs. Bergheim and family, (Mr. B. is the chief of the city's bankers), and spent the day with them. A Christian family—intelligent, well educated, and exceedingly agreeable. The sad sight, and yet that which gave joy to the whole house, was the three dear little children who lost their father so tragically : one a darling baby of eleven months old, born a month after the father's murder. The mother and her two eldest boys are now in England. Spent a most delightful day, and left for my hotel, accompanied by a servant with his lamp, after Scripture reading by one of the sons and prayer by Mr. Bergheim, senior, who is in sadly shattered health, and I don't think will ever get over the shock of his son's terrible end. On our way to the hotel we saw a bridal procession, with many lamps carried by many friends. The bride wore a long white dress that completely covered her, and a veil of silver strips and spangles. There was singing at intervals, but no music, and little talking. The bridegroom was not there, but was waiting the arrival of the bride at his house in the Armenian quarter, on the outskirts of the city.

November 22. Spent an hour or two on the Mount of Olives ; visited the church (Latin) built by the Princess Latour d'Auvergne, Duchess de Bouillon, and the schools instituted by her. The place is chiefly remarkable from its having been built close to the traditional site of the Ascension—overlooking Bethany on one side and Gethsemane and Jerusalem on the other, and being, it is stated, the actual place where the Saviour gave His

The Gate of Bethlehem

disciples the prayer bearing His name. Suitably enough, the Lord's Prayer is engraved on large tablets round the inner square in twenty-four languages, and at the side is a tomb, with a marble recumbent figure of the Duchess, destined for Her Grace when she leaves this world for another. Coming down the Mount, we went into the oldest Christian church, said to be built over the remains of the Virgin Mary, and consequently held in high repute by the Eastern Churches. In the afternoon went to Bethlehem with the Bergheims—the busiest as well as the most interesting place I have yet seen outside Jerusalem. Everybody seemed engaged, and there was much building going on, and everything to indicate prosperity. The streets, of course, are narrow and dirty. Exquisite engravings on mother-of-pearl are produced here in great numbers. Mrs. Lawson showed me two for which she had given 120 francs each—the subject, the Lord's Supper—in which the expression conveyed by the engraver was as perfect as if on wood or copper. Our point of attraction was, of course, the Church of the Nativity—in which, like that of the Holy Sepulchre, the Churches of the East have each their place of worship. A certain stone, which is said to mark the place of the Nativity, was the cause of the Crimean War. Who should be the custodians of the Church of the Nativity led to the endless complications that preceded and ultimately brought about that terrible war, in which so many of our noblest and best were sacrificed. The view from the large open square, where the Arab boys were playing, was very fine. All are Christians in Bethlehem—Copts, Armenians, Greeks or Latins; the Mussulmans live outside. I saw here many wives of 10 and mothers of 12 years of age. An effort is being made to prevent such early marriages, but the system is so engrained that it will be difficult to alter; unfortunately, the fact that money can be got by needy or greedy parents for their baby girls, is itself the strongest obstacle to any change. The signs of wifehood are necklaces of silver pieces hanging round and down the neck; very few of the Christian women use the veil or yashmack; those who do have it made of black crape or lace, upon which a light pattern is printed. The dress of the Jerusalem women above the peasant or working-class is a white linen burnous, which is large and entirely covers their body and head, leaving the face exposed. The olive groves are very abundant here, and form the chief support of the peasantry. Oil is of course the main object, but large quantities are exported, and, where used for oil, the residuum is dried and prepared for fuel. Fuel is the great difficulty of the place, for although fires for heating houses are rarely needed, yet for cooking they are always in requisition. There are very few trees, and no coals or peat. This leads to the destruction not only of the few trees here and there, but of their roots, which are dug up, brought in on camels' backs, and sold at so much per hundredweight. I was told that the cost is gradually increasing, as the peasants have every year farther to go for trees and roots. One serious result is that the country becomes more arid than ever, and the return of the ancient fertility of the land rendered still more unlikely. Besides roots and the *débris* of the olive, cowdung is mixed with chopped straw, dried in the sun, and stored for firing, as peat is stored in Ireland. Institutions of every kind abound here, so much so that the usual result of indiscriminate almsgiving follows. There is a good deal of pauperised feeling among the people, and backsheesh is looked upon as a respectable, as well as the usual, mode of living : idleness and all the vices too frequently follow. Still, there are here some of the noblest institutions imaginable ; perhaps the British Ophthalmic Hospital and the Hospital for Lepers are the most notable, and altogether free from objection. The London Jews' Society is doing great good, but is not cordially welcomed by either Jews or Christians : proselytism is always feared by the first and generally deprecated by the second. I visited the hospital and the work-room connected with their schools, and was greatly pleased. Dr. Wheeler presides over the one and Miss Lindsay over the other. Every country has its Consul here, so that the lives and property of Europeans are as safe as in

England. The Protestant Church is the smallest in number and importance of any ; indeed, it takes no part in the active controversies of the place. The Greek Church is the largest and most influential of the Christian Churches, then comes the Latin (Romanist), then the Armenians, Syrians, Copts, and last the Lutheran and Protestant. Jerusalem shows signs of progress —building everywhere outside, and some attempt at drainage works inside the city. Raouf Pacha is the Governor of Jerusalem, and is spoken of in terms of regard and respect by everybody. He is as little bigoted as it is possible for a Mussulman to be, but he is a Turk, and affected with the indolence and indecision that characterise his people so generally. When appointed to his post there was a promise of vigorous action, not afterwards fulfilled : he ordered inquiries to be instituted into one and another of the abuses of the city, but no report has ever been or ever will be made. There are at the present moment at least half-a-dozen current ; the last two were ordered to inquire into *who* was to inquire, and *what* " who " was to inquire about ! No beneficial result is at all likely to follow. Jerusalem is despotically governed, like all Turkish cities, but the despotism is modified to a very important extent by the influence of the consuls of the European powers ; the natives owe everything to them. In the interests of Europeans, who swarm here, liberties are secured, and insensibly this is felt and shared in by the people. A municipal body has been recently instituted. Some parts of the city's narrow streets are being repaved, and drainage operations are going on, but there is no certainty of their continuance. At any moment the peasants may be ordered to other work, or return to their villages, and the undertakings be abruptly stopped. The only water supply is obtained from rain-water tanks in different parts in and about the city. In the days of Solomon water was abundant, and still can be had in the pools he provided some two or three miles from Bethlehem, whence aqueducts brought it to the City of the King ; traces of this great work are still to be seen. Some years ago Lady Burdett Coutts offered to provide water for the people of Jerusalem under her own superintendence and at her own cost. It will scarcely be believed, but it is true, that the authorities declined to allow this to be done unless the Baroness deposited the money and allowed the Turks to carry out the work—or not—in the way that seemed to them good. To this day, therefore, the people are without water, as they are without gas or other mode of lighting the narrow streets and alleys of their ancient city. The streets are *very* narrow—no wheel carriage could go *through* any one of them, though just by the Jaffa Gate it would be possible for a line of carriages to pass. Every camel and ass is taxed to pay for the works in progress, and if this would only continue, a few years would see Jerusalem a model Eastern city. Jaffa is the chief (if not the only) port for Jerusalem, and the road between the two cities is the disgrace of the day and the Government. Gangs of men are at work, as they have been for some years past, but only a few out of the forty miles are finished. The work is done by forced labour— that is, the peasants are taken and compelled to work a certain time on the road for nothing; one excuse given for this is that it prevents the need of taxation for this special work, but, it need not be said, it gives rise to much complaint and great suffering : those who can pay backsheesh get off, whilst the very poor have to do all, without pay or food. If this road were made, and another to Damascus, there would be no reasonable limit to the progress of the country. A French company has long had the concession of the road from Beyrout to Damascus, upon which they levy tolls, and, as a consequence, trade is developing with astonishing rapidity in this far-off Palestine city. The country, despite its mountains of stone, is very fertile, and, blessed with a good Government, its industrious and patient people would flourish and prosper, whilst the land itself would become again the desire of all nations. Trees, and the produce of every tree, are now taxed, instead of unproductive land, so that whole districts that would produce the rich Indian corn, the olive, the date, and the pomegranate, are now bare, miserable, and unproductive—a very Gehenna.

23. My last day in Jerusalem, into which I have crowded a great deal. The Mosque of Omar is built on Mount Moriah, where the Temples of Solomon and of Herod once stood, over the rock, which stands up sacred and untouched, upon which Abraham offered up his son Isaac. I had to get special permission to go over this building, and had to be accompanied by an armed soldier as well as my dragoman. Only Mahomedans are supposed to enter these most revered of all places. I left my boots at the entrance, and walked through the immense courts and buildings in slippers. The mosque itself is gorgeously decorated with mosaic, but no pictures are permitted by the followers of the Prophet. The Sacred Rock stands up in the centre, exactly below the domed cupola. I went into the subterranean buildings, called Solomon's stables—evidently very ancient, if not of Solomon's days. One need not wonder that the Queen of Sheba "had no more spirit in her" when she beheld all the marvels of the Temple and of the king's house and gardens; there is quite sufficient to enable one to say the magnificence of the place must have equalled all the glories of Greece and Rome for barbaric grandeur, if not for grace and beauty. From here I went, accompanied by my guard and dragoman, to the wretched prisons of Jerusalem, in which are herded all the captured murderers, thieves, and villains of the place, some (those who are convicted of murder) in chains, all gaunt and miserable, with no division or distinction, in an open yard, with two massive doors of open ironwork through which you see the men, who come clamouring to the inner gate for backsheesh as a strange face presents itself. About a dozen soldiers, with loaded carbines, guard the outer gate, but it is not long since the prisoners broke out—many of them assassins—few if any of whom have been retaken. The guard called forward one or two of those convicted of murder : their sentence is fifteen years' imprisonment, and they have chains to their hands and

feet. One was an old, sad-looking man, who has no friends, except one elder brother, who supplies him when he can with the pittance necessary to get him food; for little, if any, is provided by the Government. At my request the coachman of poor Mr. Bergheim was called up : he is the man who is supposed to have stunned him with his club and given the first stab. He was tall, not bad-looking, a defiant sort of Arab, with no apparent fear of results. When he will be tried nobody knows : he has been in prison nearly twelve months, and when he is tried, unless he confesses—which is not at all likely—it is probable he and the other seven or eight engaged in the murder will get off. If convicted, he will be sentenced to a nominal fifteen years' imprisonment, which backsheesh, violence, or other circumstances may reduce to a few years, or even months only. A sickening sight, and, with backsheesh to the guards for the prisoners, which it is very doubtful if they get, I speedily left the place. My next visit was to the *Tombs of the Kings*—rocky excavations, very vast, and with evidences of magnificence and age which establishes their claim to have been the resting-place of the ancient grandees, if not the kings, of Judæa. They are on the north of Jerusalem, about two miles from the Damascus Gate. I groped my way into the inner chambers, in each of which there was provision made for some six bodies, with convenient holes in each for the bones to be put when time had destroyed the flesh, and so make room for others. No idea can be conveyed of the extent of these tombs, or of the labour their excavation must have entailed. An immense stone runs still on the groove cut for it thousands of years ago, which shuts up the only entrance into this vast charnel house. On my way back I called in to see the model of the three Temples—Solomon's, Herod's, Omar's—prepared with immense labour by a German gentleman long resident here. It helps you to understand the past and present buildings, and form a very fair idea of their extent and magnificence. I mistook the German lady who showed me the models for the housekeeper, and, I regret to say, offered her backsheesh, which she declined. I afterwards learnt, to my horror, that the good lady was Mrs. Schenck! When I went over the hospital and schools of the London Jews' Society I was taken down to the basement —far below the present street—which is supposed to have been the prison in which the angel appeared to Peter, and which was followed by the ever memorable exclamation of the astounded gaoler, "What must I do to be saved?" Somehow I felt this very likely to be the place tradition asserts it to be: the depth below the present roadway (called Peter Street), the ancient walls, the prison-like look, the general surroundings, and its nearness to the Tower of David, made it far less difficult to believe than much else to which I had recently been introduced. Called to say good-bye to Mr. and Mrs. Ogilvie, who had been very kind. Also upon the Bergheims, with whom I felt quite at home. The old gentleman, though never likely to be himself again, still takes much intelligent interest in everything; the sons are smart men of business, likely to increase the large undertakings their father has initiated; the daughters clever, well-read, thoughtful women; and the dear old lady, who was married at fourteen, has been the mother of twenty children, of whom nine survive, and who, despite the terrible troubles of the last year, is still cheerful and chatty, sympathising with and sharing in the pleasures of her children, and particularly kind to me. She sent her love to my wife and children, about whom I think I had been talking a good deal, and hoped God would save them from her sorrows, whilst giving them all her happiness. She is a very tiny woman, but has fine sons and daughters. Yesterday my dragoman took me to see the good woman who prepares the flowers of Judæa for sale; she was his neighbour and the friend of his wife. Here was repeated the charming mode of salute with which children and inferiors meet you in Judæa, and no doubt elsewhere in the East. My dragoman's wife, a broad-faced, large-eyed, untidy woman, kissed my hand and carried it to her forehead. At

Miss Arnott's school one dear little girl to whom I talked did the same thing, and I confess I appreciated it far more from the Arab child than from the Arab woman. As this was my last night in Jerusalem, I took another look from the roof of the hotel, and once more saw the never-to-be-forgotten panorama spread out before me, and the hills round about the City of the King. One feathery palm tree rising high up above the houses was the solitary evidence of fertility. The flat roofs of the houses, the Mosque of Omar, the Church of the Holy Sepulchre, and the domes and minarets of less important buildings, with the Mount of Olives standing up clear and bright in the light of the young moon, showed me for the last time a scene deeply solemnising, and that will be for ever impressed upon my memory. Unfortunately I cannot see Northern Palestine, Damascus, the Sea of Galilee, Samaria, and the other places sacred to the active life of the Saviour. I leave early in the morning, and cannot forbear placing upon record my sense of gratitude that I have been permitted to see Jerusalem, the place of so many hallowed memories. Although the hotel is not in every way satisfactory, its position makes it most attractive. From the windows of the saloon and dining-room the view of Jerusalem life is as attractive and remarkable, as that from the roof is impressive. The hotel juts out into the road from a kind of angle whence three streets diverge, and commands, therefore, a very diversified outlook. On one side everything entering the Jaffa Gate is seen; on the other the Street of David, leading to, or rather forming a part of, the Mount of Zion; whilst, standing on the balcony, you look to the left upon the narrow and ever-busy street down which jostling people and heavy-laden asses and camels are continually passing. Yesterday morning I watched the crowds of passers-by with intense interest. First came—led by a band of some twenty men, blowing trumpets with monotonous, but not unpleasing, iteration—the soldiers from David's Tower opposite me; some 200 stout-looking, dark-hued men, dressed very much as our convicts are dressed, with short coatee jackets, fez caps, and trousers not in very good condition, and not always of the same colour, though mostly of rough, coarse cloth, dark green and blue ; then a string of camels, varying from two to twelve, led by a single Arab, bearing roots of trees, corn, and fruits and vegetables ; asses bending under heavily-laden panniers, and often with the added burden of their thoughtless owners upon their backs. Sometimes women strode ass or camel, though, as dress and mode of riding are alike in both sexes, it was difficult to decide which was which. There are women, too, bearing heavy burdens upon their heads, and men with the grotesque water-skins and other commodities, for the busy market below ; and, by the way, I notice that while women invariably bear their loads upon their heads, the men as invariably bear theirs upon their backs; women with the white covering, which is the usual dress of Jerusalem, sometimes with the yashmak, and sometimes with their faces uncovered ; of every colour, every class, and of many tribes and peoples ; monks of the Latin Church, priests of the Armenians and of the Greeks, with their distinctive robe and head-dress : black men, brown men, white men, Jew and Gentile, Arab and Abyssinian, old and young, blind men and beggars, the halt and lame—such a motley mass of human beings, in every Eastern dress, in every variety of colour! Truly the sight here, as upon the housetop, is never to be forgotten !

FROM JERUSALEM TO PORT SAID.

24. LEFT in the early morning, about 7 o'clock, in the same carriage in which, some days ago, I had entered Jerusalem.
Very bright and beautiful ; indeed, in this, as in so many other ways, I have been exceptionally favoured. This is the time of the *early* rains, the *latter* come in March or April, and both are usually very severe, and altogether interrupt journeying

and sightseeing. I have had none, and have not been kept in one hour by the weather. I am not in the time of flowers, but then the heat would be unbearable. Although I have lost what everybody says is a great treat, yet I have my compensations. The first sad token, despite the brightness of the morning and the evidences of prosperity about me, that I was in a despotic country—where, "whilst every prospect pleases, only man is vile,"—was the sight of some fifty Arab peasants, taken from their homes for the army, roped together, and guarded by soldiers with swords and loaded muskets, tramping on their weary walk for Jaffa to ship for Constantinople. There were not wanting the natural accompaniments of the scene—wailing women with babies, and old men and women, with difficulty keeping up with the rapid march of the troop; some were noisy and reckless, others sorrowfully looking down upon the women clinging to their pinioned arms, with, let us trust, words of love if not of hope. The road, of course, was execrable, but I saw how wonderfully rapid is the growth of vegetation here. The occasional bits of rough ground amid the mountains of stone, which were in process of ploughing when I passed some nine days ago, were now showing green and promising under the influence of the life-giving sun. I passed the place where the Jew was murdered a few days since, and saw the only half-obliterated evidences of the struggle, and where poor Bergheim met his terrible end. Here and there were a mile or two of good road, with gangs of peasants, pressed, without food or pay, for the work. Some day—years hence—there will, perhaps, be a good road from the Port of Jaffa to Jerusalem, and from Jerusalem to Damascus; and when this day comes doubtless the prosperity of Palestine will be largely increased. I reached Jaffa at 4 o'clock, just in time for the Khedevial steamer leaving for Port Said. Again I realised the value of Mr. Cook's arrangements: my ticket was a return one, for use on the Austrian Lloyd's vessel which left Jaffa the next day, but thanks to the great house's representative, it was changed for one for the Khedevial boat, and I thus saved a day. What was done for me is done for others, and hence I argue that journeying in places like Palestine, Egypt, and India, is rendered by him not only possible but pleasant for even the most timid and inexperienced of travellers. Sorry I could not again call upon Miss Arnott, where, I think, a little present, prepared for and by one of Mr. Cook's *protegés* awaited me. Met my Norwegian companion again.

FROM PORT SAID TO CAIRO.

REACHED *Port Said* at 7 o'clock, too late for the postal boat to Ismailia. Went to the Hotel de France, as before; lunched there, and then called upon Mr. and Mrs. George Royle, who had returned from Malta, and who welcomed me in their beautiful home like an old friend. Had a walk with them on a slip of the desert by the side of the Mediterranean, with their dear little girl. Mrs. Royle has infinite charm of manner, as well as grace of person, and has that invaluable power belonging only to the few—(Mrs. Cook is another notable instance of this)—of making you feel at once at home; fitted to shine in any society, yet preferring above all things her home, her husband, and her child, although there is here absolutely no society, no rides or drives, and scarcely a place in which to walk. Was honoured by being made free of the nursery, where the good mistress of the house was actively engaged in the prosiest of domestic occupations, and with the same grace as that with which she afterwards presided at her hospitable table. Mr. Royle took me over the "Paramatta," a vessel of the P. and O. service just back from India. She is lighted by electricity, and has a splendid square saloon, infinitely superior to the "Kaisar-i-Hind." The coaling of all the boats of the great service is done by Mr. Royle, and is, I trust, a source of considerable profit to him. When on our ramble by the shore saw the singular traps set by the people of Port said for catching quails, which at certain seasons abound there—shrubs are set up with an opening on one side, and a wire at the other. When once in, the foolish bird has not the sense to turn, and is readily snared. Mr. Royle is a barrister, and a cultured gentleman as well as an active man of business. I hope we may see both him and his wife in London some day, though, remembering their beautiful house, I shall scarcely care to show my own modest home.

November 26. Left my hotel at 6 o'clock for the postal boat, which takes me up the Canal to Ismailia, whence there is rail to Cairo. The country is altogether different from that of Palestine. There all was rocky, arid, treeless, and mountainous; here everything is flat, sandy, and monotonous, until we reach *Agassiz*, where the influence of the Nile and its offshoots is felt, where everything is green and flourishing, with drooping palms, fields of corn, feathery grasses, bamboo, sugar-cane, and cotton, with mighty acacia trees, plantains, and bananas; small rivulets, but no hedges, walls, or other divisions to be noticed— all level, like one great open field. The flat-roofed houses of Judæa were all of stone; here they are equally flat-roofed, but built of mud and half-tempered bricks, and thatched with the reeds and straw of sugar-cane and Indian corn. The men, women, and children very busy, and apparently happy; not very particular as to their clothing, for I saw more than one absolutely naked man engaged in the work of the fields. The first part of the journey was through sandy desert, but soon after passing *Tel-el-Kebir*, the scene of the great battle with Arabi and his followers, we entered the fringe of the delta where the Nile begins its fructifying work. The camels are not so numerous and are much smaller than those of Palestine, with neater heads, and without the repulsive under-hanging jaw that distinguishes the larger variety. The ibis, the modern representative of the sacred bird of the Egyptians, I saw in great numbers, following the plough and the husbandman without let or hindrance. They are a large white bird, and their confidence is striking, as great as that of the pigeons in the Guildhall-yard at home. I saw here, in large numbers, the Egyptian buffalo, with its hump, long dewlaps, and horns like those of the goat. The water-wheels, and other primitive modes of irrigation, the *sakieh* and *shadoof*, for which Egypt has from time inmemorial been celebrated, were everywhere. For some time before reaching Cairo, which I did about 5 o'clock, I saw in the distance the Great Pyramids, far away on the horizon. The latter part of the railway journey had been through the ancient Goshen, the land given to Joseph's brethren by Pharaoh. My good friends Cook and Harris, and the ubiquitous Mahommed, were at the station to meet me, and although the place was new and strange, I at once felt myself at home. After a warm bath, which was most acceptable, I sat down to a capital dinner with a very fashionable party in the saloon of Shepheard's Hotel, capable of dining 150 people; went with my friends to see some parts of old Cairo, and some wonderful horsemanship, and thence home to the hotel, mounted upon "Bismarck—one good donkey," as the saucy little Arab boy informed me.

———>·<———

CAIRO AND THE PYRAMIDS.

November 27. MY bedroom looks out on an open courtyard, very oriental in character. There is a plashing fountain, and lofty palm trees, plantains, and a banyan tree that has thrown down many branches to take root in the ground below. The pointsetta, a tree-like shrub with resplendent crimson flowers, is very plentiful. Numbers of grey crows build in the trees, and the cawing is like to that of a park avenue or country churchyard at home. My room is but indifferently ventilated, and, with closed doors and mosquito curtains gathered round my bed, is at times almost unbearable. The view from the front of the hotel is very interesting, and one can scarcely wonder that "Shepheard's" still maintains its position, though

it is expensive, and lacks some of the advantages looked for in
first-class hotels at home. It has gardens on either side, and
a raised open front approached by a flight of broad steps from
the roadway, canopied from the sun and shaded by acacias,
and with lounges and easy chairs innumerable, on which
visitors rest whilst watching the busy and various throng constantly passing on pleasure or business bent. The Arab boys
with their donkeys, with the high crimson leather cruppers, are
the most noticeable feature ; the camels are but few ; the
carriages, when not broughams, are light open victorias drawn
by two horses, and invariably driven by Egyptians in the
universal red tarboush or fez. With Mr. Harris and Kingsford
early to the *Pyramids of Gezah.* Not long ago the only way
was to cross the Nile at Old Cairo, and thence proceed by
donkeys across fields of swamp and wastes of sand : now a fine
bridge leads to a really splendid road made by the late Khedive,
planted with acacia and sycamore trees. These celebrated tombs
of the ancient Egyptian kings—which by many ages preceded the
rock tombs that abound in Upper Egypt—are variously stated
to date from 4,255 to 2,450 years before Christ. Anyway, they
belong to an age for which Biblical chronology scarcely prepares us. They are situated on the edge of the Libyan Desert,
about seven miles from Cairo, of which, from the Pyramids, we
had a splendid view, and of the Nile and its palms, and the
Citadel and Mosque of Mehemet Ali. There are three great
Pyramids : the first and largest, that of *Cheops*, the second of
Chephren, Cheops' brother, who succeeded him, and the smaller
of *Mycerinus.* They are within the Necropolis of the ancient
City of Memphis. The larger Pyramid occupies an area of
nearly thirteen acres, its sides are 750 feet long at the base, and
its height 451 feet, much higher than the cross of St. Paul's. I
made an attempt to get to the top, but was too giddy, I regret
to say, to be able to succeed. I was attended by two Arabs,
who were more than attentive, and for a time insisted upon my
proceeding. I ascended about 200 feet, and then somewhat
abjectly begged to descend, promising—may I be forgiven !—

any amount of backsheesh upon my arrival at the bottom. M. H. did not attempt the ascent, but Mr. Kingsford succeeded, though at the expense of a sprained ankle. I went into the interior, and saw the King's Chamber and the Sarcophagus of Cheops. As the way in for some distance was only from three to four feet in height, short as I am I found it difficult work, but persevered, and was glad that, if I failed to ascend, I at least explored as thoroughly as can well be done the interior of this wonderful work of the ancient Egyptians. After resting a while, went on to the *Sphinx*, the colossal head with which we are all so familiar. It has recently been cleared of the sand, and we have now, therefore, the whole body revealed. From one point only is it like the Sphinx with which poor Benwell and other artists have made us acquainted. It is 66 feet high from its paws to the top of its head (in which, by the way, is a great hollow, into which one of our Arab guides descended for some special backsheesh). The nose is 5 feet 7 inches and the mouth 7 feet 7 inches in length; the full breadth of the face is 13 feet 8 inches. It is hewn out of the natural rock, and was probably intended as the giant guardian of this great burial-place of the kings. Although terribly mutilated, the face has a very winning look, and its grace and beauty grow upon you. We lunched at the foot of the greater Pyramid, and returned home through long avenues of acacia trees, which meet overhead, and form a splendid shady drive for the good people of Cairo. We crossed the Nile by its bridge, the Kasr-el-Nil, at either end of which two colossal lions stand up as the defiant guardians of this approach to the city. The Nile is covered with long low boats, their spars extended horizontally, and with lateen sails that look so dangerous and are so graceful.

Sunday, November 28. Went to the English Church, a plain stone cruciform building with many memorials of the brave Englishmen who have already laid down their lives and left their bones in this faraway place. The army chaplain—the Rev. T. Smith, of Rorke's Drift fame—preached what was no doubt a very good sermon, but I regret to say he had not been taught to regulate his voice, which was loud enough, but quite indistinct. When will our bishops insist that the first qualification for the preacher shall be the power to make himself heard ? The good old gentleman who read the lessons was equally unfitted for his work. How I longed for a morning at Norwood, and the voice of the preacher and teacher about whom I so often think !

November 29. Mr. Cook's new steamer is being finished for to-morrow's journey. The Khedive expressed a wish to see it, and J. M. C. is therefore away to receive his Highness. Evidently, and with reason, our friend is accepted as a great power here, and Tewfik, the present ruler, is awake to the invaluable services rendered to his country by the enterprise of the great house at Ludgate. To the *Boulak Museum* with M. H. Had my first experience of what donkey boys can be if you have no dragoman. Upon attempting to get a donkey, one among a dozen or more, I was literally run down by the whole troop: the picture of the fight in the Black Forest for our carcases and our luggage was what a skirmish is to a pitched battle. I was seized by half-a-dozen at least—run at, run down, and run over, and was glad to rise and flee for my life. Fortunately I found a solitary Jerusalemite round the corner, and was able to join my friend M. H., who had wisely taken one away from its brethren, from which some other adventurous traveller had just alighted. *Boulak* is not far from Cairo, and is really a kind of harbour where the numerous folk engaged in the river traffic congregate. It is more oriental than Cairo, and one sees greater variety in men and attire here than elsewhere. The great printing office of the Government, which I had no time to visit; the Egyptian arsenal, and the large engineering works are situated here. The Museum is deeply interesting, but, like all places of a similar kind, is excessively fatiguing, and, without more time than travellers usually can give to it, somewhat unsatisfactory. Here are sarcophagi, sphinxes, ancient shrines, enormous statues, sacrificial tablets, deities, boats (like the gondola of Naples), stone hicroglyphics, and hosts of other evidences of the immense antiquity, artistic power, and greatness of the people of this land of the Pharaohs. The most ancient figures carved in wood in the world are here, and mummies and mummy cases by the hundred. Here are exposed the veritable remains—horrible enough—of a line of Pharaohs, among them the one (Rameses II.) whom Moses bearded and whose people Jehovah overwhelmed. There are jewels of priceless value and fabulous age found in the mummy cases of queens and princesses recently discovered, who lived and loved and passed away thousands of years before the Christian era. We took a carriage drive through the city after our exhausting visit to the museum, and saw the fashion of the city, who regularly drive through the avenues surrounding Cairo, and the racecourse, which English officers have laid out and support. Here I saw the ladies of the harems of the princes and pashas, with their repulsive-looking guardians, the eunuchs. The bright eyes and fair faces could be plainly seen beneath the transparent veils which more than half revealed the charms of the houris of the East. To the citadel, and mosque and tomb of Mehemet Ali—a magnificent building, whose graceful minarets can be seen everywhere in and about Cairo. Here the founder of the present race of Khedives rests after his troubled life : a great man, bold, brave, vindictive, and treacherous—notably was this last characteristic shown by his massacre of the Mamelukes in 1811—who, but for us at Acre, would have made Egypt independent of the Sultan, and been the first of a new race of Egyptian kings. Saw an Arab school—all the dirty little fellows squatting on the ground and droning out passages from the Koran. The Tombs of the Mamelukes are very picturesque, looked at from a distance, but near at hand they are but ruined records of the eventful past. The Desert is encroaching fast, and a century or two will leave those who come after us but few evidences of the character of these relatively modern sanctuaries of the dead.

FROM CAIRO TO LUXOR.

November 30.

UP betimes and on board the "Prince Abbas" by ten prompt. This is one of four splendid steamers just built by Messrs. Cook and Son for tourist traffic on the Nile. She is 160 feet in length, has two decks, draws only 2 6 feet of water, and will accommodate, besides her captain and crew of 38 men, 32 first-class and 30 second-class passengers. The appointments are most complete, and in character will vie with the best of the P. and O. boats. Although our ultimate point is the first cataract, the first day is arranged to be a picnic to *Sakkara*, enabling certain of our passengers to return this evening to Cairo, while the rest of us proceed on our journey. Those who only go so far are the guests of Mr. Cook—among them we have Mr. and Mrs. Walter, jun., of the *Times*, Mr. and Mrs. Lawson, Mrs. and the Misses Gordon, who came with us in the "Kaisar," General and Mrs. Wilkie, and one or two members of Parliament, and important men connected with railways and the Government here. Soon after leaving we passed the *Island of Roda*, which is believed to have been the place where Moses was discovered by Pharaoh's daughter (whose mummy, by the way, is to be seen at Boulak). There are remains of ancient palaces here and there, but the island is now virtually a busy suburb of Cairo, with plenty of houses and gardens of the well-to-do. We stopped at mid-day at *Bedrachan*, and took donkeys for the site of ancient *Memphis*, the *Pyramids of Sakkara*, the tombs of the Sacred Bull, and the *Temple of Oonus*, which latter has been cleared out at the expense of Mr. Cook. The great statue of Rameses, said to be 50 feet high, lies in a swamp, from which the waters have not retired, so we only saw the back of the great man's head. The hieroglyphics in the Temple of Oonus are remarkably perfect, and show the ancient Egyptians engaged in the labours of their day—in no way different from those of the present time. Labour even high artistic labour, must have been very cheap in those days. Never earthly monarch had nobler sepulchre than was accorded the Sacred Bull by the Egyptians. No wonder its worship had attractions for the newly-enfranchised Hebrews in their desert wanderings. Mounds of broken pottery, and fragments of brick and granite, are all that remain to show the site of Memphis, the ancient capital of Egypt. As our desert journey altogether was one of some fifteen miles, and we had besides to climb up hills and crawl down into tombs, we all returned fairly tired to our home in the "Prince Abbas." Our picnic friends returned to Cairo in the "Khedive," a sister vessel, while we proceeded on our journey.

December 1. December! and such a gloriously fresh and luminously bright morning! I don't wonder that only strangers talk of the weather : here it is unvarying and always alike beautiful. Comment on the unchangeable becomes monotonous, and is not practised by the natives. Last night we had secured ourselves to the Nile banks at *Ayat*, but my old enemies, the dogs, aided by the crowing of cocks and the cackling of hens, kept me awake half the night. Dogs and cocks are outwardly like those creatures in England, but with a difference. With us there are times when dogs don't bark and cocks won't crow, but here there is no cessation to their irritating noises. It doesn't at all signify that the dog has no earthly reason for barking— no foe, human or canine; he just barks on, morning, noon, and especially night, for mere cussedness : whilst the cocks care for neither sun nor moon, but cackle and crow from sunrise to sunset and from sunset to sunrise. Surely dog and cock ought to be articles of modern Egyptian as well as ancient Greek faith and worship. Had a quiet day steaming up the Nile, passing innumerable villages with ever the evidences of the fertility of the fringe of land upon the Nile banks, the industry of the people, and the presence of the barren and sandy desert beyond. The palm trees, so graceful ; the mud huts, so characteristic ; the people, so busy, so strange, and so dirty. The universal and only dress of the women is a long loose gown of dark green or black ; the children, boys and girls, naked, or with the barest of apology for dress ; the men barelegged, turban-covered and loosely clothed—and the number of all uncountable ! Camels are comparatively few, but the patient donkey and the useful buffalo are in great numbers, and in no part of our journey are they lacking on the river banks. The sugar-cane, the Indian corn, and a kind of semolina, growing some twelve feet high, and the ever delightful palm, varied with patches of tobacco, cotton, rice, and a kind of clover, are the principal crops—the extent of which can always be seen from our vessel's deck. In some places the desert comes down to the Nile banks in sandstone rock, when of course no cultivation is possible; and nowhere since we left Roda have we seen much more than half a mile of cultivable land saved from the desert. On either side of us these deserts stretch—the Libyan to the right, the Arabian on our left. There are immense sugar factories here and there, some of them still and likely to remain unfinished. They were the ill-considered undertakings of the late Khedive Ismail, and they show his recklessness and unwisdom in a very marked way. We were to have seen the working of one of these, but unfortunately it was closed and would not be opened until the new year. We are now at *Maghaga*, a large village 100 miles from Cairo.

December ?. We unmoored at 6, and reached *Gebel-el-Dayr*, on the left bank of the Nile, about 11 o'clock. A strange-looking mud-built convent, belonging to the Copts, the Egyptian Christians, was shown us at the top of the hill—differing in appearance very little from the square hovels of the villages we had passed. Whether the priests pray and preach and practice well, I don't know, but they are said to be dexterous swimmers, and, until the custom was stopped by the Patriarch at Cairo, were wont to swim out to the passing *dahabiehs* to solicit backsheesh for the support of their convent. We reached *Beni-Hassan* (170 miles from Cairo) early enough to visit the rock tombs of the kings and generals of ancient Egypt. We went on donkeys—such a cavalcade ! Every donkey had at least two attendants—bare-legged, bright-eyed, laughing lads of from ten to eighteen; and their shouts and gesticulations, and, I am sorry to say, their very forcible incentives to movement applied to the poor asses, made a Babel of sounds not readily to be forgotten. Some of our party came to grief more than once, but I held my own without difficulty or mishap. We passed through two or three villages, where mothers with babies at their breasts were eagerly soliciting backsheesh; through palm groves and corn fields to the interesting places of sepulchre, cut out of the solid rock, towering over the narrow slip of sand and garden below. Cyclopean work, innumerable hieroglyphics, and colours as permanent as the unchanging Sphinx, are found everywhere along this range of sandstone mountains. In the evening the young folk gave us song and glee, which, varied with pleasant chat, closed one of the happiest of days spent in this delightful country. Have been suffering from sickness, but the doctor on board—Dr. Crookshank, a wonderfully pleasant companion, a gentleman who holds the important position of Director-General of the Prisons under the Egyptian Government—gave me medicine which no doubt will soon enable me to enjoy again the pleasures of the table and the still greater pleasure of the journey. My special companions, J. M. C. and M. H., most kind, of course.

December 3. Still not well. Up very early to see our start. The natives, although the morning sun had not yet risen, clustering about the banks in great numbers. Mr. Cook had distributed a bagful of copper coins among them the previous day, so the welcome of future travellers on vessels bearing the red flag of Cook and Son is assured. The doctor and Bertie shot some twenty pigeons yesterday, and occasionally bring down a vulture, cormorant, crane, or other large bird, which, however, we are unable to secure. Nothing is more interesting and novel than the numbers of large birds one sees everywhere on the Nile. A flock of more than a thousand cranes has just been wheeling in front of us, far above, in regular irregular lines, on their way for the low sand shoals, which are their chosen feeding ground. Beautiful as the sunsets are, they are speedily over, and there is no lengthened pleasant twilight as with us : to the west there will be the glorious orange glow of diffused sunshine, to be seen nowhere but here, while to the east all is dark and gloomy, unless lit by the light of the early moon. We constantly pass sailing trading vessels with their graceful lateen sails bearing the small red flag of Cook and Son. The firm has some 40 or 50 of these boats always upon the Nile, taking from or bringing produce to the Cairo market, or supplying the needs of Her Majesty's troops up the Nile. I have heard of more than one king whose revenues are less than those of Cook and Son, and I know of some dozen whose usefulness is infinitely less! We reached *Assiout* or *Siout*, the capital of the Upper Nile, about a mile from its western bank, about 5 o'clock, too late to see much of the place. Here we take some ten or twelve generals and colonels, with their wives and belongings : they have come on by rail from Cairo to this, the end of the great Egyptian line. It is something to say that Egypt has had this line, 250 miles in length, for many years, and that thus the capital of Upper and Lower Egypt are connected by rail and telegraph, with all the advantages that these civilizing means ever bring in their wake. The population of the place, I am told, exceeds 25,000, including merchants of very considerable wealth ; one—a Copt—is stated to return his income at £25,000 a year! There are at least twenty-five mosques here, with their graceful minarets, also extensive bazaars.

December 4. Up betimes, as breakfast was ordered for 7.30 to enable us to start at 8 sharp for the sights of *Assiout*. About 5 in the morning we were all awakened by the new-comers and their luggage, and at 7 I received in my cabin welcome letters from home that the train had brought from Cairo with our new passengers. Our donkeys took us to the hills behind the town, whence we had a glorious view of the city, the Nile, and the great canal, which starts from this place and continues its fruitful course right away to the Pyramids of Gezeh. There were tombs as usual—wonderful in extent and massive grandeur; some for the sacred wolves, and one for the architect who had designed the works of a king of the fourth dynasty, who flourished more than 3,000 years before Christ. The plain is very extensive here, and spreads out for some miles on either side the Nile, very green and fruitful. Under the hills, and taken from the desert, is the great burial-ground of Assiout, the most important I have yet seen, occupying some fifty acres, in which there are domed and extensive and expensive tombs, walled in, indicative of the wealth of the people whose bones lie here. The bazaars, which are, as usual, narrow ways covered in by light lattice and rushes, and with open shops, with their cross-legged owners reclining within, are numerous, and, being market-day, presented a more bustling appearance than anything I had previously seen. It was almost impossible to push our way through the crowds of people, camels, donkeys, and heavily-laden peasants. I am afraid my donkey trod on many a toe, and that I unwittingly hustled many a peaceful trader in this busy hive. Bought a few characteristic bits of pottery, but they are so fragile it is doubtful whether I can ever get them home. Before the advent of the English, this was the great slave market of Upper Egypt, but with our coming this obnoxious traffic has to find outlets farther removed from English influences. We left intending to stay at *Tahta*, about 300 miles from Cairo, but, at the request of the Commander-in-Chief of the Egyptian army, General Grenfell, one of our new arrivals, we proceeded as far as *El Maharah*, where we laid to for the night.

Sunday, December 5. A very quiet day. If a clergyman be on board, it is usual to have the service of the Church of England read, but lacking that we were deprived of any meeting for worship. The day was an idle one, but watching the natives upon the banks, the shadoofs at work, the villages on the banks, the enormous birds—storks and pelicans and vultures—with Scripture readings of the journeyings of the Israelites, and a very little talk with my companions, brought the day to a fitting close.

December 6. We reached *Keneh* last night, and started on donkeys in the early morning for the *Temple of Dendereh*. This was our first visit to one of the great Egyptian temples, and it seems scarcely possible that anything hereafter to be seen can be more wonderful. Besides its extent, its condition strikes one with wonder: it is comparatively perfect. Its outer hall consists of 24 pillars, 25 feet in circumference and 70 feet high, covered with sculptured hieroglyphics, perfect save that the Moslems have obliterated all the sculptured faces of the sphinxes, gods, and kings that crowned every side of the pillars within and without. It is contrary to their religion to have the human face depicted, and, although they have become more tolerant now, when they first became owners of the country they destroyed all the noblest specimens of this form of art. Hence the condition of the Sphinx and of the many statues of Rameses and of the other Pharaohs. In this temple is a sculpture of Antony's Cleopatra, who is represented as a somewhat full-lipped woman with sensuous face, and likely therefore to be a portrait of that dangerously fascinating beauty. We descended into the Treasure Chamber far below the great hall, where, although out of sight and necessarily rarely visited, we find the same elaborate carvings, and the same colouring as on the walls of the temple above. Here we met with bats innumerable, who extinguished the candles, and caused some commotion among the ladies of the party. A very enjoyable day, leaving food for thought as long as memory lasts. Reached *Luxor* early in the evening. Here is a first-class hotel in an extensive garden facing the Nile. It belonged until quite recently to Mr. Cook, and has all the comforts of Cairo and Alexandria. We are moored close to the Temple of Luxor, whose massive columns stand out on the moonlit sky, grand and awe-inspiring. Mahommed made our arrival at Luxor a notable event. He lives there, and this was his first visit after his pilgrimage to Mecca, which gives him the title of Hadji and

Effendi, entitling him to wear the green turban, and to become ever after a man of importance among his people. In addition, this was the first coming of the first of the new line of steamers, and the result was a very interesting reception, and a sight rarely to be seen. Our vessel was dressed from stem to stern with flags of all nations; at the prow were two splendidly decorated green flags bearing the Prophet's monogram, and with texts from the Koran, while two small cannon were run out on either side, and loaded for the *feu de joie* which was to announce our coming. The excitement on board, as on shore, was very great: Mahommed was dressed in his green turban, silken robes, and green sash: our passengers were all assembled at the prow, and we saw flags everywhere on the buildings along the shore, and gathered masses of men and boys. Our cannon were fired again and again—six times; and from the Consulates of England, Germany, and America guns were fired in response. As soon as we were moored, a number of the priests and sheiks came on board, each in his turn saluting Mahommed thrice on either cheek. Banners and flags and beating drums, and troops of men and boys were waiting on the banks, and after he was nearly torn to pieces in the embrace of his kinsmen and townsfolk, preceded him to his house in the town. His three boys were the first to meet him, but of course his wife remained at home to greet her lord, whom she had not seen for five months— Moslem etiquette not permitting her appearance in the streets. Mahommed, who is a man of some wealth, had bought his wife a pair of gold bracelets—very heavy—made of English sovereigns, and worth more than £20. Open house had to be kept by the hadji, and free entertainment afforded to all comers. We were specially invited to come round in the evening. About 9 o'clock, therefore, with the moon shining brightly over the temple and the town, General Grenfell, J. M. C., M. H., and myself wended our way to the house of the great man. As we came near we heard the monotonous chanting of the Moslem effendi, who were reciting passages from the Koran, and accompanying themselves with the everlasting tomtom, pipe, and zither. On either side of the narrow street—the widest though in Luxor—were benches covered with rich carpetings and cushions, upon which some fifty or sixty Mussulmans were seated smoking their long narghilas and drinking sherbet and coffee. A seat of honour had been reserved for us opposite the entrance to the house (one of the best in the town, though the casements were without glass, an article little seen in Upper Egypt), and sherbet, cigarettes, and coffee were successively handed to us by smartly-dressed and swarthy Arabs, who bore the various refreshments upon plated salvers, over which richly embroidered covers were thrown. Mahommed was very busy with his guests; and from above we could see just sufficient movement at the lattice of the windows to show us that the wife of the hadji, though forbidden to take part in the entertainment below, was busy with friends of her own sex, and could watch the animated scene in which her husband bore the chief part. Meanwhile sheep were being prepared for the more substantial feast which was to follow. We afterwards learnt that fourteen sheep were consumed in two nights, and that poor Mahommed was not freed from his too devoted guests till four in the morning. We left after many expressions of goodwill, Mahommed kissing the hands of the General and Mr. Cook, and shaking hands with the rest of us, while the sixty or seventy old gentlemen with their pipes rose and saluted us with all gravity, and two or three Arabs accompanied us with large swinging lamps to our ship. All this, Mahommed told us a little dolefully, would continue as long as we remained in Luxor.

December 7. We crossed the Nile, which is very wide here, in boats to the opposite side to visit *Thebes*, where are the grandest and most extensive of the wonders of ancient Egypt: the Tombs of the Kings—excavations exceeding 24,000 feet in extent; the Colossi, 60 feet high, the only two remaining out of eighteen, which originally led up to the Temple of Amonuph; the Memnonium or Ramesium; the Palace of Koorneh; the Temple of Amonuph III., and the vast Temple palace of Meeden-et-

Columns of Temple at Luxor.

Haboo. For this we take two days, very tiring, but, needless to say, delightful and interesting. Here the Arab peasants, men and women, girls and boys, were trying to turn a more or less honest penny by the sale of real and sham antiques— mostly sham ones, manufactured at Luxor on the opposite side —and the gruesome mementoes of the long-buried dead : hands and arms and feet swathed in the mummy clothes of long ages ago. I bought the well-preserved hand of a woman who had lived when Joseph became second to Pharaoh and the saviour of the people. One gets to feel that, though we have something yet to learn, our mode of sepulture is less objectionable than that of the ancient Egyptians. "Dust to dust," "ashes to ashes," the rapid mingling of the remains of poor humanity with its parent earth, is far better than to be thus embalmed and kept for thousands of years, to be at last disentombed by unhallowed hands, for purposes of gain and for the gratification of the morbid taste of savants and travellers. Ours is a large party, and we had, besides the curiosity sellers, a crowd of donkey-boys, girls carrying water-bottles, and hosts of mendicants, blind men and beggars, and lazy Arabs, who live by begging and backsheesh. The little girls were very pretty, and patiently ran by our side all the day, looking for a piastre or two when the day was over. We had one troublesome fellow who followed us everywhere, playing a species of double flute, which gave forth, without alteration or change, about a dozen of the vilest of the notes one gets from the Scottish bagpipes. It was evidently highly appreciated by the natives, and the performer was looked upon as a great genius, but to us it was maddening : the first day we tried threats, and, I think, by one of our party, a young lieutenant, blows, but that had no effect : he was up and smiling the next day, more persistent than ever. We then tried backsheesh on a liberal scale, but this made him frantic, and we had the greatest possible difficulty in keeping him from our boats when we returned in the evening. On the second night, the first having been spent at Mahommed's reception, we were invited to the house of the son of the

English Consul, an Arab, to drink coffee and witness the performance of the dancing girls of Luxor. All such entertainments are called *fantascias*, Nearly all the gentlemen of our party went, together with Mrs. Calvert and Madame Portalis, two of our lady passengers. The room was large and long, roughly plastered, and with cushioned seats all round, except at the end, where a number of men and women were crouching—the men playing the tom-tom and a kind of single string violin : very monotonous, as usual. Two dark women, with bright eyes and not unpleasing features, came forward and began a singularly ungraceful dance, throwing their bodies about in a way impossible to describe, and that seemed to violate all the laws of anatomy. They had long loose dresses, an embroidered girdle high up under their arms, and naked feet, and accompanied themselves with brass castinets. The exhibition was not agreeable, though I should have been sorry to miss it. Sometimes, I am told, when in certain company, and under the excitement of drink, the performers are very objectionable; but what we saw, apart from its ungracefulness, could not be complained of. One woman danced with a lighted candle in a bottle on her head, for perhaps fifteen minutes, throwing herself about in a most extraordinary manner, but without displacing the candle. Our host was obsequiously polite, and sent us to our ship accompanied by a dozen servants bearing lamps.

December 9. We started for *Karnak* early in the morning, through the town of Luxor, with its busy people and dirty narrow streets. A good deal of building is going on, and no doubt its excellent hotel and its many advantages will make it a popular place for Egyptologists as well as for the ordinary traveller. Karnak is about 20 minutes' ride from Luxor, with which place it was originally connected by a roadway 65 feet in width, and with a magnificent avenue of sphinxes more than two miles in extent, the sphinxes but twelve feet apart. Karnak is more than a mile in circumference, and consists of five outer gates, approached by avenues of sphinxes (magnificent

Propylon at Karnak.

in the extreme), and many temples, erected by various kings, their innumerable pillars (some thirty feet in circumference), with the courts and sanctuaries, still standing. The Nile is supposed in very ancient times to have taken a more easterly direction, making the whole series of temples, tombs, and colossi —*Karnak*, *Luxor*, and *Thebes*—one great city of temples, avenues, palaces, and tombs. Very evidently there was an avenue of gigantic sphinxes that passed down in front of the western approach to Karnak—the remains, even now, being more than a mile in extent—and that probably originally crossed what is now the Nile, joining the Memnonium on the other side. We ascended the propylon, and had a view for ever to be remembered. All around were the enduring monuments of Egypt's ancient greatness and present decay—massive pillars, walls, and monoliths, adorned with hieroglyphics of their kingly builders and chronicles of their reigns. The enclosures connecting the entrance gates were probably originally of earthworks; but the temples are all of massive stone, bearing the records of many dynasties, and the result of many centuries of labour. One obelisk, far larger than that on our Embankment, bears upon it an inscription proving it to have been cut from the quarries at Assouan, more than a hundred and forty miles away, sculptured, dragged here, and erected by Queen Halesa, of the 12th dynasty, in the space of seven months! The walls abound with many historic records, but none more interesting than a sculptured portrait of Rehoboam, king of Judah, whose fenced cities were overwhelmed, and whose treasures and holy vessels were taken by Shishak, of which we have a short but graphic account in 1 Kings xiv. Strange to say, although we have all sorts of evidence of who the people were, how they lived, the power of their kings, the battles that were fought, the mode of quarrying sphinxes, pillars, and monoliths, and how they were removed from their rocky homes, nowhere have we anything to tell us the way in which the immense blocks of stone used in the erection of the temples were lifted into the elevated positions they now occupy. There must have existed some mechanical force now unknown to us, the secret of which is, apparently, never to be discovered. In the evening we went again to Karnak to see it by moonlight. I suppose that we all shall remember the glorious sight as long as life lasts. General Grenfell and Mr. Budge—the latter a gentleman from our British Museum—made some extensive purchases : mummies, tablets, gold chains, stone gods, beads and rings in endless numbers, taken from the tombs of the kings and priests, with which the Theban Valley is full. Mr. Budge gave £12 for a mummy in its much-adorned outer case. Its destination is the British Museum. It is one of the most perfect obtained for some time, and contained all the usual decorations and trinkets.

December 10. Visited the schools of the American Mission, and heard the boys and girls read and sing. They are taught English and Arabic, and the Scriptures are read and expounded. The Mahommedans do not object to the reading of the Bible by their children. Their great prophets are Adam, Noah, Abraham, Moses, Jesus, and Mahomet; and they accept the older Testament, with some modifications, without demur. Upon the arrival of the postal boat, with despatches for General Grenfell and Mr. Cook, nobody else being blessed with letters, we left Luxor at 12.30. On reaching *Esneh* we visited its small but very perfect Temple by light of the moon and the more prosaic lamps of our Arab attendants. Plenty of people in the town, and the usual rows of open shops in the narrow places called bazaars. There is a large prison and barracks here, and the Egyptian troops turned out to do honour to General Grenfell.

December 11. We reached *Edfou* about 9 o'clock, and directly after breakfast started on donkeys for the Temple. This is not so extensive as that of Dendereh, but, though of an earlier age, is quite as perfect, and as it is under the guardianship of a Government officer, no beggars are permitted inside, and we were enabled to look over its marvels without interruption from the troublesome mendicants and their eternal appeals for backsheesh. The view from the roof of the great entrance-hall was very fine, and as

The Temple at Edfou.

we looked down immediately upon the village of Edfou, we saw the primitive character of the homes of the fellaheen, mud-built and covered with reeds and sugar-cane, and something too of their domestic habits. About 3 o'clock we passed *Gibel Silsilah*, the great quarries whence all the stone for the temples was obtained in the far-off ages. There are blocks remaining, partly quarried and cut, the completion of which was probably stopped by some now unknown political convulsion. We left early in the afternoon, and reached *Kom Ombo* about 4 o'clock. The temple is picturesquely situated upon an elevation, and looks down directly upon the Nile. Some forts have been built here, commanding the valley on either side; and in the evening, when we visited the ruins by moonlight, we were challenged by the Egyptian sentries, who appeared to be but half satisfied with our polyglot responses—no wonder, seeing that Arabic was not one of our acquisitions.

Tombs at Beni Hassan.

Reached *Assouan*, the present limit of Upper Egypt, at the foot of the First Cataract, about 9 in the morning. We have now reached the Nubian Desert. We are nearly 600 miles from Cairo, and the whole character of our surroundings has changed. Instead of low-lying plains, a wide river, and more or less distant sandstone hills and sandy desert, we find ourselves in fairyland—in the midst of a hundred rocky islets, surrounded by picturesque hills of granite, porphyry, and basalt, with groves of the mimosa, acacia, and palm, with flags flying from minarets and temples, and a crowd of Arabs of every tribe and colour—Turks, Negroes, Abyssinians, and Moors—attracted by the cannon that heralded our coming. Egyptian soldiers, in their white dress, black belt, and red tarbouch, line the banks; whilst officers of the English and the Egyptian army, in varied uniforms, but all with the white helmet of the East, come on board to welcome General Grenfell and the other military men who are among our passengers. This is where our forces have been for the past twelve months, ever since their withdrawal from Wady Halfa. This, too, is where the great work of provisioning and transporting the army was seriously commenced by Mr. Cook in our late campaign in the Soudan. Everybody knows what that work was : 11,000 English and 7,000 Egyptian troops, with 40,000 tons of stores, were conveyed from the railway terminus at Assiout to Assouan, and thence to Wady Halfa, at the foot of the Second Cataract, between the middle of September and the beginning of November, 1884,—together with 800 row-boats, from Alexandria to the same place. For the accomplishment of this, 28 large steamers were chartered from the Tyne to bring 40,000 tons of coal, of which some 25,000 tons were consumed; 13,000 railway trucks were in use between Alexandria and Assiout, 27 steamers were employed on the Nile day and night, and nearly 700 sailing boats of every tonnage. Besides all this, an army of more than 5,000 of the fellaheen of Upper and Lower Egypt were in the constant pay of the firm, superintended by more than 150 Europeans of different nationalities. This is the first time in our history, probably, that any such work has been entrusted to a private firm, and the way in which it was successfully accomplished and all difficulties surmounted is an imperishable monument to the house of Cook and Son ; and one wonders that, amid the lavish disposal of honours and dignities, our friend J. M. C. should have been left among those

Grottoes of Silsilis.

unrecognised and undecorated. We rowed across to *Elephanta*, an island opposite Assouan, where there was, however, but little to interest us save the *Nilometer* (there is another at Roda), cut in the unchanging rock, to mark the rise of the Nile. Upon the extent of the rising of the river depends the measure of prosperity of the fellaheen, and the amount of the taxation to which they are exposed ; a low Nile means lessened crops and reduced taxes. If honestly used, not an unfair mode of assessment. Afterwards we took a hurried ride through the bazaars and streets of Assouan, and returned to our steamer to dinner. The evening was spent in the singing of Hymns Ancient and Modern, and we were favoured by the Misses Calvert with some of Beethoven's exquisite sonatas.

13. An idle day. We strolled through the town, visited the bazaars, bought some pipes, and took a short journey upon the railway constructed for the English troops, to save them the difficulties of the First Cataract. Here, as elsewhere, the flies are an intolerable nuisance to us Europeans, though apparently in no way objectionable to the Egyptians ; the dirty little children, whether on their mothers' shoulders or tumbling in the dust, being literally eaten up by the flies without a protest on their part or any effort to rid themselves of their tormentors.

14 A number of camels and donkeys were gathered on the banks for our ride through the Desert to the upper part of the First Cataract and to *Philæ*, a lovely little island upon which some beautiful ancient temples stand. I never tire, by the way, of looking at the camel—that misshapen quintessence of orientalism. Whether singly or in long lines, as they are seen most frequently, they always strike me as the comic survival of pre-Adamite days.* On this occasion I tried a camel, but

---

* "The long bended neck apes humility, but the supercilious nose in the air expresses perfect contempt for all modern life. The contrast of this haughty *stuck-up-ativeness* with the royal ugliness of the brute, is both awe-inspiring and amusing. No human royal family dare be uglier than the camel. He is a mass of bones, faded tufts, humps, lumps, splay joints, and

soon betook myself to the humbler donkey. The uncouth noises of the animal I bestrode, and what seemed to me his vicious tendencies, culminated when he set off down a very steep hill at a disgustingly unpleasant trot. I kept my seat, but with some difficulty. I induced an excellent young fellow, Behrens, the banker's son, to exchange his donkey for my camel, and I was thus enabled to enjoy the rest of the journey, which was very interesting. We passed on our right the sad evidences of the price we pay for the thankless duty we have undertaken in Egypt : a square enclosure, surrounded with a neatly-kept mud wall, containing the graves of the poor fellows who have fallen victims to the climate and the attendant hardships of their location here. Very bright were the white headstones, mostly surmounted by crosses painted in black, with the roughly cut

---

callosities. His tail is a ridiculous wisp, and a failure as an ornament or a fly-brush. His feet are big sponges. For skin covering he has patches of old buffalo robes, faded, and with the hair worn off. His voice is more disagreeable than his appearance. With a reputation for patience, he is snappish and vindictive. His endurance is overrated—that is to say, he dies like a sheep on an expedition of any length, if he is not well fed. His gait moves every muscle like an ogre. And yet this ungainly creature carries his head in the air, and regards the world out of his great brown eyes with disdain. The sphinx is not more placid. He reminds me, I don't know why, of a pyramid. He has a resemblance to a palm tree. It is impossible to make an Egyptian picture without him. What a Hapsburg life he has ! ancient, royal ! The very poise of his head says plainly, ' I have come out of the dim past, before history was ; the Deluge did not touch me, I saw Menes come and go ; I helped Shoofoo build the Great Pyramid ; I knew Egypt when it hadn't an obelisk nor a temple ; I watched the slow building of the Pyramid at Sakkara. Did I not transport the fathers of your race across the desert ? There are three of us : the date palm, the pyramid, and myself. Everything else is modern. Go to !' His strange grunts and groans frighten or pain you, according as you are led to believe they are the consequence of anger or suffering. When you find the same uncouth sound proceed from him, whether loading or unloading, whether beaten or caressed, whether walking, trotting, or standing still, you realise that his ways are peculiar and the reason of them past finding out. All that can be said of him—and it is much—is that he is the only possible beast of burden in arid, sandy, and desert countries, and that here in Egypt he is invaluable."—*Moslems and Mummies.*

inscription telling of "somebody's darling" lying below. I saw only the names of privates and non-commissioned officers, and presume, therefore, that the officers, many of whom also succumbed, lie elsewhere. All around were desert and rock, and our hilarity was checked for a time by the thoughts the sight suggested. We passed through one or two Nubian villages—similar but somewhat better than those we had before seen : the men, women and children, black as negroes, but many with handsome features, and all the men tall fine-looking fellows. We saw several wild-looking Bichareens on camels ; they are Bedouins and true nomads, never living in towns or villages, with their long platted black hair, curled fantastically, and without any covering to their heads. Our most interesting visit on the way was to the granite quarries, whence all the obelisks, sphinxes and figures of that material, found everywhere in Upper and Lower Egypt, have been obtained. There still remains an immense block, originally intended, it is thought, for an obelisk, partly cut out of the rock by the fellaheen of the days of the Ptolomys, and that now stands exposed to the wondering eyes of us moderns in this nineteenth century. Our destination was *Shellah*, opposite Philæ, to which latter island we were taken in row-boats flying the flag and with the boatmen bearing the name of Cook and Son upon their gaberdines, very handsome-looking fellows, who kept time with their singularly interesting but somewhat monotonous chant, consisting of meaningless sentences ending with passages from the Koran and ascriptions of praise to Allah, and Mahomet his prophet. There was a shout at intervals, in which visitors as well as boatmen joined. After inspecting the magnificent columns and temples of Osiris, we lunched in an ancient kiosque, somewhat fancifully called Pharaoh's Bed. Excavations and clearings are going on here under General Grenfell's directions, and one trusts they may be carried on to completion. Arab mud hovels have been built over priceless treasures of architecture and art, and when they are removed the Island of Philæ, if only because of its matchless position and its traditional site as the burial-place of Osiris, the most prominent of the Egyptian demi-gods, will prove the great point of attraction for all interested in the wonderful remains of ancient Egyptian civilisation. When the Egyptian mythology ceased as a system of religion, and the early Coptic Christians gathered on the Nile, there was an important colony here : we see, therefore, plenty of evidences that old hieroglyphics were defaced and Christian symbols substituted. The cross and the palm, and forms of the Trinity, are very frequent, and in one corner of the great court there is a recess where evidently the Christian altar once stood. After lunch our boatmen were ready to row us down to the Cataract, or as nearly thereto as they dared without danger. We landed, ascended a neighbouring hill, and then saw what everybody has read of : the shooting of the rapids by the natives. I shall never forget the sight. Lithe, tall, black fellows, naked, or with an occasional covering round their loins in deference to our susceptibilities, leaped into the rushing waters, amid very frightful-looking rocks and boulders ; some upon logs of the palm tree ; some with uplifted staves, upon which fluttered rags bearing verses from the Koran, or flags of English manufacture. Tney were swept unresistingly down to a point far below us, where their vigorous efforts enabled them to land. Again and again was this repeated, and then came the fight for backsheesh ; howling, screaming, gesticulating, as only wild men can do, they rushed upon us, and it was only by a free use of the stick, and the dexterous efforts of Mahommed, that we were relieved of our enemies. We gave liberally, and returned to our boats somewhat "touzled" by our engagement. When returning, through the rocky islets everywhere, we realised something of the difficulties of the way : all the efforts of our boatmen were powerless against the rushing waters ; we were swept back again and again ; and it was only when half a dozen of our fellows plunged into the waters, and with ropes attached to their bodies dragged us, whilst the remainder bent sturdily to the oars, that we succeeded in heading the current and reaching

The First Cataract.—Shooting the Rapids.

our landing-place, at a village called *Mahattah*. Here the donkeys awaited us for our return journey, which we made along the picturesque banks of the Nile, and in view of the rapids and cataracts. There is a railway from Assouan round the cataract to Philæ; this we had availed ourselves of the day before; but on this occasion we used the pleasanter mode of travel—donkeys and camels. Mr. Cook invited all the officers stationed here and their wives to dinner and a dance on board. Great preparations were made, and for the first time on the Nile a steamer was found large enough to entertain a party of fifty to dinner, with ample room for music and dancing afterwards. We spent a very pleasant evening, not a little of our enjoyment being due to the never-failing geniality of General Grenfell, whose knighthood and whose position and dignities did not prevent him from heartily joining in all the amusements of the evening; who was ready to sing a song, join in a glee, tell a tale, dance a saraband, and make himself the general helper of all; and also to the wife of the commissariat officer stationed here, Major Skerwin, who gave us a scene from the "School for Scandal," and other recitations, with great power and much taste. I hear the lady is an authoress, and was married at Cairo very recently under somewhat romantic circumstances. At the close of the entertainment, one capital fellow, an officer who wore the Victoria cross, and many another evidence of his bravery and pluck, rose to propose a vote of thanks to Mr. Cook. He was not, however, as expert with his tongue as with his sword, for he very speedily forgot his purpose and his host, and assured us with effusion that he was delighted to entertain us, was prepared to receive us in the same hearty way on any future occasion, and concluded by telling Mr. Cook that he was as welcome to the Nile, to Assouan, and to the ship, as though they were all his own!—and he meant it! —yet the real modesty of the man was as evident as his bravery, but like so many of us, he was "unaccustomed to public speaking." I am told the troops are to be withdrawn before the hot weather sets in, for sanitary rather than political reasons, and although the place is strikingly attractive to a stranger, I doubt not they will gladly hail the orders which take them back to Cairo or Alexandria.

FROM ASSOUAN TO ALEXANDRIA.

December 15. A VERY early visit to the tombs recently discovered and cleared by General Grenfell. Among his many other accomplishments, he adds that of being an earnest, generous, and intelligent Egyptologist, and has devoted his money to the clearing of the very ancient tombs that line the rocky hills facing Assouan. Ours was an unusual treat : we had the General as our cicerone, and Mr. Budge (who has been sent out specially by the British Museum) as our interpreter. The most important of the tombs already cleared was that of the chief officer and friend of one of the kings of the fifth dynasty— a time which takes us back to the days long before Abraham left his Chaldæan home. From the elaborate inscriptions upon his tomb, he appears to have been a compound of Commander-in-Chief, head of the church, Prime Minister, and personal friend of the Sovereign he served, and was permitted to add the king's name to his own. He appears to have been lame, and to have united his son with himself in the cares of government. An attempt was made to photograph us at the entrance to the tomb, but I fear with but poor results. The General accompanied us to our boats, and we parted with him as from a friend of long standing. He is on his way to Wady Halfa, where the Soudanese are causing some anxiety to the Egyptian Government, though the English officers and General Grenfell do not anticipate anything very serious as likely to arise. " The Prince Abbas " had steam up, and started directly we arrived for our return to Cairo. As she goes down stream at the rate of sixteen miles an hour, our journey back will be very speedily accomplished. We reached *Luxor* and moored for the night about 7 o'clock.

Columns at Karnak.

16. Another ride to *Karnac*, another attempt at a photograph of a group in which I am one, a stroll through the town, tea in the hotel gardens, dinner at 7, and some games and music afterwards, finished another delightful day. The ladies had been invited to visit the Hadji's wife, and were much pleased with Mrs. Mahommed and their reception. They described her to us as being rather handsome, somewhat sad-looking, a little coquettish, and apparently a spoilt wife; dressed and decorated with rich embroidery and many necklets, bracelets, charms, and trinkets. Her face was coyly covered at their entrance, but after a time she unbent completely, removed the rich shawl with which her head was enveloped, and showed her rich dark hair, plaited, oiled, and decorated with charms and rings. She is about 32, rather *petite*, and very engaging in her manner. The visitors were regaled with sherbet and coffee, and returned delighted with their glimpse of the inner life of a Mahommedan home of the middle class.

17. We started early, and reached *Keneh* about 10 o'clock. Here, again, we had donkeys, and rode through the town and bazaar, and saw the potters at their interesting work. One never tires of watching this, the earliest of the arts, and never ceases to wonder at the rapidity with which charming forms rise under the manipulation of the deft fingers of the workman. Keneh is a busy town, fairly clean, and the people bright-looking and handsome: the women, with their babies perched crossways upon their shoulders, less anxious to hide their charms (perhaps because they are better worth showing), and the children, it struck me, less dirty than those of most of the towns we have visited. The dust and flies are, as usual, intolerable. There are barracks, a prison, and several important-looking houses in the public square. The gendarmes are here—the force which is under the command of Colonel Valentine Baker; they were dressed in their blue regimentals, and were a smarter class of men, I thought, than the soldiers we saw at Assouan. After resuming our journey, we passed belts of the dome palm—trees breaking out, some ten feet above

the main trunk, into four or five branches, each with a graceful date-bearing head. We reached *Bellianah*, where we stay for the night, sufficiently early for some of our party to go through the town, chiefly remarkable for its many pigeon-houses and the bad character of its inhabitants. Dr. Crookshank, who is, I think I have mentioned, the Director-General of Egyptian Prisons, told me there have been more rows, robberies, and murders here than in any other town on the Nile. We had passed it on our upward journey without stopping, and it is the only town of any importance we shall visit on our way down.

December 18. A very tiring day. The gong sounded at 6 o'clock. Breakfast was over, and we were in the saddle by 7 o'clock, and away to visit *Abydos*. Our road, after passing through Bellianah, was through fertile fields of green crops, presenting a more English-like appearance than any we had noticed on other of our journeys. Extensive fields of beans and a kind of clover and sanfoin, besides the usual large plantations of doora and sugar-cane, with palms and mimosa here and there. A few of the villages had a pond and open space in the centre, in which hogs, geese, pigeons, and turkeys were fraternising, having something the appearance of an English farmyard. The temples at *Abydos* are dedicated, like those at Philæ, to Osiris and Isis, and consist of seven sanctuaries, in which King Sethi chronicles in various forms his devotion to the god whom some traditions say lies buried here, and his own successes against his enemies. It is very rare to find any purely unselfish Egyptian temple : with the exception of the palace of Rameses at Medinet-Haboo, in the Theban Valley, we have no permanent record of the character of the homes of the ancient Egyptian kings ; they built their houses for time, their temples and tombs for eternity ; but everywhere, in temple and tomb, the greatness of the monarch is chronicled. If the gods of Egypt are honoured, the doings of the worshipper are sculptured for the admiration and envy of his successors. This is notably seen in the Temple at Abydos. Sethi was the father of Rameses II., a king of the 19th dynasty, who flourished when the Israelites

were the bondsmen of the Egyptians, and his tomb is found in the rocks above Thebes. Six of the seven sanctuaries are dedicated to the god Osiris, but each is full of the exploits, battles, victories, and glories of the king, all of which are ostentatiously paraded before the figure of Osiris. In the Seventh Sanctuary it would appear that Sethi had turned from his faith, and, like Nebuchadnezzar, called upon his people to make him the object of their worship, for his image takes the place of Osiris, and bears the emblem of the god; and the votive offerings of captives and their riches are made to him and the spirits of his ancestors. The figures are both in basso and alto-relievo, and are more perfect than any we have seen elsewhere. In many of the courts the colours are as fresh as though done but a few years since, whilst some have evidently never been finished: they stand out white and colourless, as on the day the sculptor abruptly ceased his labours. In this temple we find the earliest specimen of the arch in Egyptian architecture, which, it is evident, Greeks and Romans borrowed from the older people. On our return journey we saw the mirage—lakes and trees and islands, clear and distinct; but changing and vanishing into the distant desert as we neared the pleasing picture. The way was long—perhaps 16 miles in all—and the sun was hot, so that all were glad of the quiet of ship-board. I rested in my cabin, after a late lunch and a hot bath. In the evening we had some charades and round games, in which Mr. Philpot and the young Calverts distinguished themselves.

Reached *Assiout* about 7 o'clock, where Mr. Cook's second steamer, under the superintendence of Mr. Cook's youngest son, who left our steamer at Luxor, was upon her upward way. Mahommed parted with us here: he will be the dragoman from Assiout to Assouan and back during the season. He is a universal favourite, and we shall all miss his, "I beg your pardon, ladies and gentlemen"—the formula with which he always began his announcement, after dinner, of the engagements of the following day. The "Tewfik" is full,

Mr. and Mrs. Locke King being among the passengers. I envy them the pleasures of the next fortnight, especially if the scenes and places are as novel to them as they were to me. Here I received letters from home—such a welcome budget; and here I heard, from Mr. Cook, that Mr. and Mrs. Lyman are not coming out in January. What a pity! How they would enjoy the trip, and how all would enjoy their company. We parted from our sister vessel amid the waving of flags and the firing of cannon. 'Tis our last day on the Nile, and what a wondrous river it is! Well may it be said that Egypt is the gift of the Nile, for not only are the fertile banks its work, but the Delta itself is the result of the alluvial deposits, made during untold ages, brought down from the rich and distant lands of Central Africa by this creative river. It is some 1,800 miles in length from Khartoum—city of poor Gordon's massacre—where the waters of the Blue and White Nile mingle, to the Mediterranean, and during all its tortuous course it acknowledges but one tributary, the *Utbara:* it gives ever, and receives never. It slowly rises from June to September; it as slowly falls from October to May. The rise in fortunate years is 42 feet, which means prosperity for the fellaheen and plenty for the Egyptian exchequer. When a higher or lower Nile marks the year, there is more or less of suffering and distress among the people and their muhdirs. The outlets into the Mediterranean once were many; now there are but two, the *Rosetta* and the *Damietta.* The river is absolutely unique; no other can make the remotest claim to any of its many peculiarities. Like Egypt among nations, so is the Nile among rivers.

As we run some 150 miles in the course of the day, we pass the towns and villages very quickly. About 9 o'clock we are opposite *Minieh,* one of the largest of the towns on the Nile. Here the Khedive has a palace, and some immense sugar factories; here are also a Coptic church of some importance, a barracks, and a prison. The Nile is a great highway, and one is struck with the immense numbers of

native boats—all with the graceful lateen sails—the luxurious
dahabeas, stern-wheel steamers, and other craft, which
come and go on its busy waters; the *shadoofs* and *sakiehs*
are everywhere actively moving; the first worked by the toiling
naked peasant proprietors, the other by the patient bullocks on
their ceaseless round. The river has fallen considerably since we
went up a fortnight since. There are islands of sand here and
there where none existed before, and green blades of young
corn where some days ago the waters flowed; where we saw
the fellaheen breaking up the irrigated soil, we now see the
tall doora stalks, whilst the forward growths have become
ripened corn. The immense fertility and speedy maturing of
everything here are truly wonderful. The singing of "Hymns
Ancient and Modern" was our only evening engagement. It
was interesting to see that, with hardly an exception, all knew
and all took part in these beautiful Christian melodies.

20.   Reached *Cairo*. Arrived at our landing-stage by the Kasr-
el-Nil Bridge at 10 o'clock. One feels a little *triste* now that
this memorable trip is ended, and that, with an occasional
exception, we shall never again see the pleasant acquaintances
we have made. There is so much social friendliness
excited when one meets in a confined space the same
folk day after day, that it often seems, when the hour of
parting comes, that we are leaving friends of long standing.
The separation, however, in this case is not quite complete—
some go with us to "Shepheard's," and many promise further
meetings. I received, for example, the card and a pressing
invitation to visit, in Paris, Mons. and Madame Portalis,
two of our passengers: he is an *ancien député*, and a Director
of the *Messageries Maritimes*. Mr. Behrens—young and
rich—and his travelling companion and coach, C. B. Philpot
(an Oxonian, and a splendid fellow physically and mentally),
threaten "to look me up" in town; Dr. Crookshank, I certainly
shall see again: the important position he holds here he is
likely still to hold, despite the jealousies of many who should
be among his sympathising helpers; Mr. Calvert is a young bar-

rister, who politely hopes some day to practise before me—and so on, and so on—everybody kind, complimentary, and sorry that the time for separation has come. During our entire journey nothing has occurred to mar our pleasures; all has been merry as the marriage bell. The weather has been, as it always is, beautiful beyond telling : the sunsets and sunrisings—and I have seen them all—and the glorious moon and stars, shining as they never do with us, are things to stand out bright and lasting on the page of life. When not visiting the temples our time has been spent in pure idleness— eating and drinking, reading, writing and chatting, with games, music, and whist in the evening. Our meals have been sumptuous in quality, and plentiful in quantity. Breakfast at 8.30, lunch (really a mid-day dinner) at 1, tea at 4, dinner at 7. I have usually joined the whist party, and left the young folks to their own devices. It would not be quite true to say I shine as a whist player ; I forget trumps, I lead the wrong card, I head my partner's trick, I keep the ace till 'tis useless, and do everything indeed that I should not do—except, perhaps, revoke. J. M. C. bears with me with a quiet patience which says much for his forbearing temper ; but M. H., who is accustomed to express himself strongly, insists that I am the very worst player the gods ever made : 'tis rare, he says, to be able to tell when one has found the worst or best of anything or anybody, but as a whist-player he is ready to stake a thousand preference shares of the L. C. and D. R. against a china orange that my equal cannot be found! With all this, we are splendid friends, and when I would join the other passengers in the saloon they hang on to the skirts of my gaberdine and won't let me go. Among our passengers was an American, a dealer in lumber in Philadelphia, who could boast that he had travelled a hundred thousand miles in the past few years. He had a dreadful note-book, in which we know all our peculiarities and foibles are chronicled, and he had the disagreeable habit of measuring, with a yard stick carried by him, all temples, pillars, and monoliths, and calculating the amount each would make if cut into scantlings! His opinion upon most things was at everybody's service, but there were few who seemed to value it when given. He was not half a bad fellow, but was certainly not a fair representative of the great American people.

December 21. I don't altogether like Cairo : its mosquitoes, if nothing else, would prevent me from willingly staying here for any length of time. My bedroom is far better than before, but my tormentors, despite curtains and eucalyptus oil, have marked me in a most disagreeable way. My right eye is that of a prize fighter, whilst my forehead bears marks usually accompanying a violent attack of small pox. 'Tis true the passing crowd, when one lounges upon the broad front of Shepheard's, shaded by its magnificent acacia trees, is novel and interesting, and not to be equalled by the view in any other city in the world— but I don't feel well here, and that spoils everything. The donkey-boys are in especial force—besides which there are the endless crowds of men of all nationalities, in their picturesque dress ; itinerant pedlars, jugglers, snake charmers, Arabs with performing monkeys, and all the host of nondescripts that gather about the doors of the evidently idle and the apparently rich. The running footmen are a great, though waning, institution. Before the carriages of the pachas, the higher functionaries, and the ladies of the harem in their close carriages, one or two tall dark Nubians, with long wands, dressed in white baggy trousers, richly-embroidered jackets, tasselled fez and naked legs, run, shouting, to clear the way. However fast the horses trot, the Syce are ever to the front. We drove to-day to *Heliopolis* (*On* of the Scriptures), the place where Joseph obtained his first wife — a few miles from Cairo. The only records of the ancient city are one monolith, but half above the ground, and a wide waste of old earthworks and abandoned excavations. It is in the very centre of the *Goshen* of the Israelites. On our return we visited the reputed tree and well of the Virgin mother, and an extensive ostrich farm, over which one of the three proprietors — a French gentleman — obligingly conducted us. There are here some 800 of these immense birds, from 4 months old to 4 years, beyond which age they are not so valuable for the purpose of feather-producing. The value of a full grown ostrich is perhaps £10, and the produce of the annual crop of feathers from £12 to £14—each of the large white wing feathers fetching four shillings, bought in quantities at the farm by the merchants, whilst those from the tail are less valuable. The eggs are incubated in great boxes, around which hot water is kept at a carefully regulated temperature. The period necessary is about forty days, and after the first fourteen it is seen whether the eggs are likely to be productive or not. The feathers are plucked every May from wings and tail—not a very pleasant operation for the poor bird—those from the wings of the male being the most expensive. The body of the male is black, of the female a dark grey. They are fed three times a day with beans and grass, and once a day have a plentiful supply of water; the cost of this must be considerable, and it is hardly possible that the profit can be great. They are by no means ungraceful in their movements, and we were much interested with our inspection of this, to us, novel industry. I called upon Sir Evelyn Baring, our representative here (introducing myself as a Magistrate of Surrey and as a Member of the Common Council of the City of London). He was kind and most polite, and readily agreed to ask His Highness the Khedive to receive me during my stay. Sir Evelyn's house is a large one in the Ismailia or modern quarter, and there were gathered the many attachés and military hangers-on that are usually found wherever our great country's representatives reside. In the evening I received a note from Lord Vaux of Harrowden, Sir Evelyn's Secretary, appointing Wednesday at 11 for my interview with the Khedive. To the Hippodrome with J. M. C. and M. H.; this is the only public form of dissipation always open to the people of Cairo, and I must admit it is of the mildest possible order. The Opera House is available but a part of the year.

December 22. Just returned from my interview with the Khedive. Sir Evelyn Baring was not quite ready to receive me ; I therefore had the pleasure of a few words with Lady Baring, who, I was surprised to learn, had never seen Assouan or been farther than Assiout in Upper Egypt. I went to the Ab-Dean Palace in Sir Evelyn's carriage, with running footmen preceding us, and my own carriage following at a respectful distance. The Cairo Palace of the Khedive occupies two sides of a handsome square, in which there are barracks and other public buildings. There is nothing Eastern in the character of the building, and it is scarcely worthy to be the abode of royalty. I was struck with the quiet character of everything : two soldiers only at each entrance—no fuss or parade. Neither the dress of the attendants nor the furniture nor appointments had any of the splendour we usually expect to find in the abodes of Eastern potentates. The carpets were more numerous and perhaps of brighter colours than those seen in Buckingham Palace, but the gold and gilding were in no way pronounced. Nor was the Khedive himself an exception to this simplicity. We were met at the entrance hall by a smiling gentleman in frock coat and tarbouch ; we were passed on up a noble flight of stairs to two others similarly attired and similarly smiling, and were received by the Khedive, whose dress and headgear were the fac-simile of that of his attendants, except that, whilst their coats were buttoned, his Highness showed his waistcoat and simple gold watch-chain. No star, or order, or other adornment, to show that we were in the presence of the ruler of Egypt. He was alone, and shook hands warmly with Sir Evelyn and with me upon my introduction, with a very winning smile. He led us to the upper part of the handsome room in which he received us, giving me the principal chair, seating himself beside Sir Evelyn upon the sofa close by, and at once made me feel quite at my ease. I expressed myself honoured with the opportunity of an introduction to the ruler of a country in which our interests and sympathies were alike concerned— spoke of his sons, and their recent visit to our country—

of my hope that some day he would honour London with his presence—assured him that, if so, the City would be prepared to afford him a hearty welcome—told him, in reply to his questions, that I admired everything in his country save the mosquitoes—advised him to raise an army of those creatures, and promised him, if they only punished his enemies as they did his friends, the recovery of the Soudan in one campaign! To all this and a good deal more his Highness replied smilingly, and entered very freely into general conversation—spoke affectionately of his sons, of the advantages of travel, of Mr. Cook's steamers, and, at some length, of the difficulties connected with the slave trade—said it was a question of labour and money; show them that the needed work could be done as cheaply with free labour as with slave, or that in any way it was to the general advantage to abolish the institution, and he had no doubt that far beyond his own dominions the objectionable trade would be extinguished. Coffee and cigarettes were handed me and Sir Evelyn Baring—the coffee in an exquisite bit of china, like an egg cup, in golden frame. His Highness neither smoked nor drank: he speaks English very fairly, but evidently prefers French, in which language he talked to Sir Evelyn. After some fifteen or twenty minutes' pleasant gossip, he rose and accompanied us to the head of the grand staircase, where he shook hands and expressed the pleasure my visit had given him. He is the eldest son of the late Khedive Ismail, whom he succeeded upon his deposition; his mother was a slave, and became the fourth wife of the Khedive some time after the birth of her son. He is somewhat below the middle height, healthy-looking, rather stout, with a short dark beard, slightly sallow complexion, nice honest eyes, and a very pleasant unassuming manner, not devoid of dignity. Very delighted with my *tête-à-tête* with royalty. Sir Evelyn most polite, and expressed himself anxious to do anything in his power for my pleasure. I should like to have been able to add to my Diary the graphic account, by a well-known writer, of the circumstances attending the deposition of Ismail and the accession of Tewfik. It showed the nobility and magnanimity of the father and the modesty and filial love of the son. Unfortunately the volume is on the "Prince Abbas," in the library J. M. C. has provided for his passengers. With all Ismail's faults, I confess to a "sneaking" fondness for the man, and to a feeling of regret that he should be added to the long list of "monarchs out of business." After my visit to the Khedive, went with J. M. C. and M. H. to the house of M. Rostovitz to lunch, though the lunch proved to be a dinner of many courses, exquisitely cooked and served. Rostovitz Bey (for he has had that dignity conferred upon him) is at the head of Mr. Cook's establishment in Egypt, and had the general direction of the recent Nile Expedition. His house is in the suburbs, and is surrounded with a large garden, in which the pointsetta and the palm, the orange and the grape, our English rose, and other beautiful flowers and plants abound. A very extensive aviary, 150 feet in length, and fountains and kiosques diversify the grounds.• In the stables were four horses, that would not disgrace Hyde Park in the height of the season. The house, however, and its contents were the most remarkable. Elegantly furnished, and with a suite of three rooms containing literally priceless Egyptian antiques and curiosities, arranged in perfect taste; with paintings, carvings, and inlaid cabinets, bronzes and statuettes, marble-lined bath-rooms, billiard-room, stained glass windows and hanging lamps—the whole establishment struck me with amazement. Everything showed wealth, taste, and artistic susceptibilities; and the thought that all this had been obtained by the fortunate owner whilst in the service of Cook and Son proved the generosity and wealth of the firm, and doubtless the unequalled services of M. Rostovitz. We were waited upon by handsome Nubians, in the very elegant dress invariably worn by the servants of the great. One particularly interesting feature of the place was the frequent appearance of the portraits of Mr. Cook and his family upon the walls and elsewhere in this beautiful home. The family grouped; each member of the family separately;

Mr. Cook thoughtful; Mr. Cook hilarious; Mr. Cook at full length; Mr. Cook at half length; Mr. Cook in oil; Mr. Cook in water; Mr. Cook etched, sketched, and photographed—everywhere one saw that the good Rostovitz appreciated, respected, and loved every member of the family from whence came his honours and his fortune; and most heartily I know does J. M. C. appreciate the faithful services and immense energy of one who has become his friend as well as his coadjutor. M. Rostovitz received from the Khedive the dignity of Bey, in connection with his work on the Nile, and finds himself rich enough to retire from the firm—which he is about to do—at an age when many men are in the heat of the battle. Long may he live to enjoy the fruits of his labour and the respect of his friends!

December 23. A day with donkeys and donkey boys. The donkey here is no better treated than elsewhere, but he has some peculiarities which make him noticeable. He is not unfrequently fancifully shaved, and coloured with henna and ochre; he has a handsome saddle cloth and highly embroidered crimson pommelled saddle; he is often adorned with silver chains and bells, and is the very quintessence of patience and good temper. The boys (of any age from 10 to 20) are most amusing fellows—quick-witted, clever and good-natured, invaluable to the stranger, never rude, and always obliging. Three times did I engage these useful bipeds and quadrupeds, and very glad am I that I did so, for I saw more of Cairo and its peculiarities than would have been possible in any other way. Cairo is being rapidly rebuilt and fast losing its Eastern character. The *Moskey*, a narrow street more than a mile in length, was, a year or two since, the great bazaar of the city, roofed in with light lattice work and full of strange, old-fashioned overhanging roofs and picturesque lattices, that are now only to be found in the bye-ways. These bye-ways—the true bazaars of Cairo—I went through from end to end. So quaint, such bits for painters and architects, such queer people engaged in such queer trades, all out in their open stall-like shops, in the full view of every passer-by. How I got through without mishap is a wonder to me ; to say nothing of other donkeys coming and going, and heavily laden men and women, there were occasionally loaded camels, and long barrow-like carts drawn by mules or donkeys; and as the wares of the traders were laid out upon the narrow ways, and the people were innumerable, it was little less than a miracle that I passed through without causing or receiving serious injury. To the donkey boys, always good-tempered and intelligent, all was due : their "arwa" "arwa" cleared the way, and brought me in safety to my hotel.

December 24. *My last day in Cairo.* General Wilkie kindly invited me to accompany him to see the trooping of the Queen's colours in the great square in front of the palace in which the Khedive received me the day before. The General is the Commandant of Cairo, and as I stood at his side I saw everything and shared in the salute he received as the troops marched past. It was a very brilliant sight. "Rule Britannia" and "God Save the Queen" were played by the band ; and I felt at home, and very proud of my country and her defenders. The General expressed himself strongly upon the question of short-time service, and the immature lads who are sent here to suffer and to die; and everywhere, from Sir Evelyn Baring down to the least important of Europeans, I heard the same opinions expressed : our want of wisdom in the past, our folly in not announcing a protectorate after Tel-el-Kebir, and the madness of giving up our present position—which is suggested by some at home—to be at once taken by our French neighbours, to the incalculable injury of the country and the people. Backsheesh and jobbery in high and low places alike have been very largely stopped; the revenues reach the Treasury intact; the fellaheen find life possible, and there is distinctly the promise, though a distant one, of peace and prosperity for this sorely tried people. After an early lunch, I went with M. Poulet, one of our recent companions on the Nile, to an old mosque in Old Cairo, to see the howling dervishes, who go through their "antics" every Friday. Like many other things one would regret not to have seen, it was a sight one would certainly not care again to see. The place was a round, lofty, dilapidated building, with a few passages from the Koran upon the walls, straw matting over the earthen floor, and partly covered with an inner circle of sheepskin mats. Under a slightly hollowed recess a young dark-skinned Arab, clothed in a plum-coloured gaberdine, with a green turban and sash, led the devotions, if devotions they were. At first only about a dozen ill-clad beggar-like looking men came in and knelt upon the sheepskins, and began, following their leader, to utter uncouth sounds and move the body to and fro; but very soon others joined them, until there were some forty in all who took part in the proceedings. After moving the body to and fro and from side to side in a kneeling position, they stood up and repeated the same movements and ejaculations. Their groans and shoutings were uncouth enough, but when three or four (one of them a boy of ten) commenced beating tambourines and tom-toms, the movements and groanings were horrible beyond telling. They gradually divested themselves of their turbans and upper garments, and their long dark hair moved in unison with their bodies, and from moans and groans they proceeded to maniacal shoutings that disgusted where it did not frighten. There were, perhaps, twenty or thirty visitors, who were expected to give liberally as they retired. There are also dancing dervishes, but as they exhibit at the same hour in another place, we did not see them. There is, however, but little difference between them—the one dances less and howls more, the other howls more and dances less. After leaving the dervishes we drove round what is called Old Cairo, to the east of the city, a part deserted and fast returning to the original desert: here is the oldest of the mosques, in a miserable state of decay, and with miserable surroundings; remarkable for its hundreds of columns, and for one in which our dragoman pointed out in the vein of the marble the names of "Allah" and "Mahomet," and which is considered of miraculous origin. We saw also the oldest Coptic church, in which were some exquisite inlaid woods, and a pulpit said to be as old as the religion itself. Visited in the afternoon the Esbekieh Gardens—a place about four times the size of Russell Square, open free, except in the afternoon, when a trifling fee is charged. There is a small lake in the centre, and kiosques and cafés for loungers. There are two or three very fine banyan trees, which but for careful pruning would soon cover the gardens— as it is, one has some dozen massive trunks besides the parent one. Left Cairo by train at 6 o'clock, reaching the Khedivial Hotel, Alexandria, at 9.45.

Christmas Day. First impressions of Alexandria : that I am once more back in Europe and have altogether left the East. Everything is French, except that there are few trees and no boulevards : French placards and French advertisements, French houses and French shops, French names and French goods, French grisettes and French cafés—everything French, but tempered here and there with Eastern yashmak, face and fez. To the English church, charmingly decorated with green climbing plants and the crimson flowers of the pointsetta and the English rose. A congregation of well-to-do fellow countrymen, the service musical, the anthem worthy of an English cathedral, and the sermon suitable for the day and clearly and impressively given. M. H. and myself afterwards went by rail to *Ramleh*, about four miles from Alexandria, to the house of Mr. and Mrs. Caillard, where Mr. Cook is staying. Our host is the Director-General of the Egyptian Customs, and we were so warmly and hospitably received by both husband and wife, that Christmas Day away from home was made—what I never expected—more than endurable. Evidently this is one of the chief centres of princely hospitality in Alexandria. Thirty-two sat down to dinner, and among the guests were the Rev. Mr. Davis, the clergyman to whom we had listened in the morning, eight or ten officers of the army and navy, a judge—Mr. Hills, son-in-law of Lord Justice Grove—and three or four high Egyptian officials and members of the International tribunals here. After a sumptuous dinner, the host, his daughter—a lady-like and very clever girl of 16—and some five or six of the guests presented a charming musical farce, distantly suggestive of Gilbert's "Ida" and "Iolanthe;" dancing followed, which I hear only ended with morning light. We returned by a special train, and reached our hotel between one and two, having promised to lunch in the same place on the morrow. The house is handsomely furnished, occupies an immense area, is on one floor only, and the rooms very large and very lofty, with a hall running through the house some 15 feet wide and 80 or 90 feet in length, lined with divans, and abounding in Turkish carpets and other Eastern adornments.

Sunday, December 26. Spent the day with Mr. and Mrs. Caillard; strolled through the desert about Ramleh, where we saw the low broad tents of the Bedouins; visited the new and handsome house of our hosts, into which they enter on New Year's Day; walked along the borders of the bay, and afterwards went with J. M. C. to the railway station at 5.30 to see him off to Cairo. He starts again on the 28th for Assouan, and will return in time to receive his family on their arrival from home. Shall never forget the constant and unvarying kindness of my good friend. Notwithstanding his enormous business, and the constant demands made upon his time and attention, we were always thought of and our every want anticipated. Life has its troubles, and one meets with disagreeables and ingratitude now and again, but happily we meet also with untold kindness, alike unexpected and undeserved.

December 27. The "Mongolia," the P. and O. boat in which we return, is just telegraphed; expect to leave some time to-morrow. Drove round Alexandria; not much that is remarkable besides the so-called Pompey's Pillar standing on elevated ground just outside the city, the Pharos lighthouse at the entrance to the harbour, and the Mahmoudi Canal, constructed by Mehemet Ali, costing untold moneys and 30,000 lives! The public buildings everywhere very handsome, French or Italian in character. The great square in Alexandria, where the massacre occurred so recently, is in course of reconstruction, and when finished will be worthy of a great city. The noble equestrian statue of

Mehemet Ali has no equal in our country, though it reminds one of Richard Cœur de Lion's that Marochetti designed at the time of the Great Exhibition. The bay is extensive, and deep enough to receive large vessels close to the wharves and jetties built out from the land, but the bar outside the harbour effectually prevents the entrance of ironclads or other dangerous craft. In the evening dined with Halton Bey, the Postmaster-General, at his club, with three or four other gentlemen, all of whom we had met at Mr. Caillard's. I have especial reason to thank my good friend Edwards for his introduction to his nephew : every attention has been shown me, and M. H. and myself were made members, for the time being, of the really magnificent club overlooking the great square. The dinner was sumptuous. We left before 12, and our host and the Rev. Mr. Davis accompanied us to our hotel. We had rain yesterday and to-day, which, with a slight shower at Cairo, is all we have had since leaving London. Alexandria and the coast line are exceptions to the rest of the country : rain is not infrequent, and although there is little beside salt swamps, lakes of brackish water, and barren wastes of sandy desert, this aridity does not arise from want of rain. *The Delta*, as a whole, is very rich, as everybody knows, but the northern coast line is an exception to the general fertility. Alexandria owes its prosperity, which is considerable, to the fact that it is the great African port, the meeting-place of Eastern and Western civilisation, and "the Emporium of European, Asiatic and African commerce." The Mohammedan conquest and the Cape route destroyed for awhile its former glories, but the present century has seen the return of more than its ancient prosperity, and its population and its imports and exports are increasing at a marvellous rate. Its population exceeds 300,000, whilst its annual exports are nearly £15,000,000, and its imports nearly £10,000,000 sterling.

FROM ALEXANDRIA TO VENICE.

December 28 to December 31.

LEFT Alexandria at 10.30 for the "Mongolia," which is to sail at 12 o'clock. Cook and Son's agents attend to everything, and Halton Bey drove down to say farewell. We had heard a capital account of Captain Fraser, and were glad to be especially introduced to him by the Bey. As M. H. at once told the captain that he had been advised to put off his journey home for a week rather than not come by the "Mongolia," and I said that I was less selfish, and only came to take the command in case of the captain's illness, we were at once upon good terms with the head of the ship, and found ourselves placed exactly opposite him at lunch. If, therefore, we are not troubled with *mal de mer* we are sure of every attention and a pleasant voyage.

Alas, for me! for thirty-eight hours I have suffered all the miseries of the middle passage. We have but fourteen passengers, so that M. H. and myself have each a cabin intended for three, and this affords the only alleviation to our lot. With oranges and beef-tea I vainly sought relief, but it was not until I tried champagne and biscuits that any came. We reached *Brindisi* at 10.30 on the 31st. There is nothing very remarkable here; its ancient glories are represented by a graceful Roman marble pillar with a highly ornamented capital, overlooking the harbour, and the ruined base of another; and its present importance is owing to the bi-weekly visits of Her Majesty's mails. Brindisi is situated a little way up the heel of the boot that appears on our maps to be trying to kick Sicily further into the waters of the Mediterranean. We strolled through the town, went up its Strado Garibaldi, through its market-place, and into its cathedral—nothing of any particular interest. In the church the service was proceeding, and we saw two miserable-looking women confessing their sins on either side of an unctuous-looking priest, let us hope with some comfort to themselves as well as pecuniary benefit to their father-confessor. Immensely struck with the essential differences of our present from our recent surroundings : rain and mud and fog; people dull, inactive, and unpicturesque; no camels or asses; no life and bustle; no cry for backsheesh, though beggars were not wanting. We stayed at Brindisi long enough to take in cargo for Venice, consisting of the oil of the olive and the grape of the vine, as well as large quantities of figs in their beehive-like straw packing, and left about 6 o'clock.

Saturday, January 1, 1887. The first day of a New Year. May our gratitude equal our mercies, and the future be more useful and more blessed than the past! Dull and cold. The wind nearly due north, and the sea high and boisterous.

Sunday, January 2. Dropped anchor in the lagunes before *Venice* about 4 o'clock in the morning; the channel is too narrow and complicated for large vessels by night. About 6 o'clock a pilot came on board, when we raised our anchor and proceeded on our way. Here and there on the wooden posts defining the narrow channel were wooden structures, like small sentry boxes, in which were poor figures of the Virgin for the spiritual comfort of the mariners. Fishing boats, with their strangely painted sails, we passed in large numbers, with an occasional trading boat and vessels of larger tonnage. It was nearly 10 o'clock before we finally anchored off the Square of St. Marco and saw in all its beauty Venice, the city of story and song. The Custom House officers kept us more than an hour before they presented themselves, and then made themselves as objectionable as possible. A duty of 36 francs was demanded for the case of cigarettes bought for George in Cairo : as I learnt in time that I should have to pay duty again in France, and once more in England, I decided, though sorely against my will, to sacrifice the cigarettes rather than pay the duty. 'Tis a mistake to bring exciseable articles through *three* countries—'tis even doubtful if it be wise to bring them to be subject to the duties of one. We parted with our genial captain, who had told us "droll legends of his infancy," and proved altogether a capital specimen of the "Captain Reece" of the

Mercantile navy, worthy to claim cousinship with him of the
"Mantelpiece." We were taken in the black, funereal-looking
gondola to our hotel by the agents of Messrs. Cook and Son.
Nothing is more disappointing to visitors on their first arrival
than the dismal appearance of the much-talked-of gondola.
Long ago, to stop the extravagance of the citizens when the
Republic affected the frugal virtues, orders were issued that
black should be the colour of the gondola, and from that day
to the present the custom is observed, though the owners of
private boats, by the adoption of tasteful liveries and the golden
badges of their house upon the sleeve of their boatmen, with
shawls and wraps of brilliant hues, correct the mistake as far
as possible. I don't venture a description so much better
given in the guide books, besides everybody knows how unique
and strange, and, when the weather is fine, what a beautiful city
it is. There are some ninety small islands, chosen as the
homes of those who fled from the Goths in the early ages,
covered with buildings, connected with bridges, 365 in number,
and between which run more than a hundred canals.
With the exception of some squares or campos, the ancient
burying-places of the people, and the great Square of St. Mark,
the whole place is intersected by narrow courts and alleys—
more than 1,500 in number. On either side of the Grand
Canal, which by devious course almost intersects the city, are the
palaces of the old Venetian aristocracy, many of them celebrated
in never-dying story, now sadly dilapidated and bearing the
unmistakable evidences of neglect and decay. The campaniles
and churches are very numerous and very beautiful—that of
St. Mark unapproachable. Some campaniles are quite out of
the perpendicular, indicating the yielding nature of their foundations.
The Churches of St. Georgia and Della Bella Saluta
stand out bright and glorious in their white marble fronts and
superb domes, rising up from the waters, the principal if not the
only buildings upon the islands upon which they are erected. We
took a stroll after lunch. 'Tis but my second visit to Venice,
the bride of the sea, but M. H. is quite at home here, and

comes again and again to its beautiful shores with all the enthusiasm of a boy, and with the cultured enjoyment of one who has made its history his study and delight. A Mr. and Mrs. Heward, who were with us a part of our journey on the Nile, and who were two of the fourteen on the "Mongolia," accompanied us, and together we saw the Church of St. Mark's, the Doge's Palace, and the Bridge of Sighs—"a palace and a prison on each hand." Mr. Heward is a stockbroker, and, with his wife, greatly added to our pleasure in Egypt, and to our later and less agreeable journey from Alexandria. They are both good—good in every sense of the word—so entirely in accord with all that is thoughtful and devout, and yet with such intense enjoyment of all the little pleasures of life, that I feel myself a distinct gainer by their companionship. We were unfortunately too late for the only English service, and this made me more than ever miss my Sundays at Norwood, and the pleasures connected therewith. Oh, for the sensitive face and absolutely perfect utterances of my dear teacher and friend, Mr. Tipple—and a sight of Deacon Bell, whose very presence makes an atmosphere of love—and Father Pritchard, with the prominent nose and Puritan face, and his dreadfully solemn announcement of even jubilant hymns, yet with such a depth of wisdom, affection, and humour lying not far away, ready to show themselves upon the slightest provocation—and my magisterial brother, Heath, the perfect gentleman everywhere—and quiet Captain Woods, whose very gentleness if the sea were but reasonable would rule the waves and still the storm, however high the winds might blow! Well, though my enjoyment is very great, it has its drawbacks, and there is something besides frost and snow and fog to look forward to on my return to our tight little island.

January 3. A day of sight-seeing, tiring, though delightful. Antonio, the principal guide connected with the house of Cook and Son, was our showman. The galleries are remarkable for their collections of the great painters of the Italian school, though other schools are fairly represented. Here are the first and last pictures painted by Titian, the first at 14, the last at 95!

Statues are not numerous, but very fine : that of Admiral Coleone stands in the Campo St. John and St. Paul, in the church of which very many Doges lie, and the plaster reproduction at the Crystal Palace shows us what that is : that of Daniel Manin, the great tribune of the people, is remarkably fine ; it is erected in front of his old home, and with the roused lion in bronze at the corner (not the centre) of the square pediment, strikes one at once with its novelty and its grandeur. Very recently, on the Quai, facing the Adriatic, a statue has been erected in honour of the soldiers who showed such devotion in 1882, when the inundations were so destructive to life and property.

January 4. My good friend M. H. very tired, not equal to sight-seeing save of the mildest order. With him to feed the pigeons, the great institution of the Square of St. Mark. They number, I suppose, some thousand or more, and daily at 2 o'clock they gather from the surrounding buildings to fight and struggle, and feed upon the corn that is regularly dispensed from one of the windows on the north-western side of the square. In the afternoon, alone to the public garden of Venice, built on two or three islands, of course connected by bridges, in which, lest the youth of Venice should be ignorant of what a horse really is, some few are kept for the officers, with an elephant and one or two rare birds from foreign climes. The place is well shrubbed with evergreens, has some pines, a fine avenue of lime trees, and a few poor statues. With our wealth of gardens and parks, 'tis, of course, nothing to note, though it must afford a welcome shade for the Venetian folk in the summer time. Here the Venice Exhibition is to be held this year, preparations for which are now being made. After this I went, in one of the little steamers which, alas ! have invaded the lagunes of Venice, to *Lida*, an island to which the good people resort as "a place to spend a happy day." It looks out upon the Adriatic, and the bathing is good. On my way I passed the island of St. Hilda, where there is an Armenian church and convent, in which Byron wrote his

"Childe Harold," and where his table and inkstand are carefully preserved. In the evening to the Theatre Goldoni, where we saw a poor representation of the *Cloches de Corneville*.

From Venice Home.

January 5. Left Venice in a snow-storm. Across the lagunes by a bridge of a thousand arches, away to the plains of Lombardy. Everything so formal—square fields, straight lines of trees, narrow dykes, plain, square farmhouses, here and there —nothing to break the dreary monotony save, occasionally, rising away to the right and left, the graceful campaniles marking the churches of distant towns and villages. Nothing to vary all this until we passed *Padua* and reached *Verona;* here there were battlements, castles, and vast fortifications, the result of Radetzky's skill, all mighty against warriors but powerless against diplomacy. Here, too, commence the mountains of the Brenner, and the railway on the right branching off to Botzen, Innsbruck, and Munich—places one knows so well. We passed through the battle grounds of nations, and reached *Milan* about 3.30, where we, or rather I, lunched, for M. H. was busy with some complications arising from railway red tape. After this, though we passed many notable places, the snow and the gathering gloom effectually shut out everything from our view. It was after 8 before we arrived at the handsome railway station at *Turin*, and past 9 before we sat down to our dinner at the Hotel Trombetta.

January 6. A thorough winter's day, snow everywhere and the promise of more. Went through some of the principal streets and squares of this beautiful city, well worthy to have been the capital of the Sardinian kingdom and the birthplace and home of the great king—Victor Emmanuel—under whom Italian unity was fought for and achieved. The squares, arcades, and colonnades are very numerous, and the statues unusually fine : that of Victor Emmanuel and of his father cannot be surpassed by any mural statuary in the world. The streets run at right angles, are broad, and the shops very numerous and handsome. One is struck with the immense number of telegraph wires which run down the sides of every street ; with the arrangements for lighting the city by electricity, the lamps suspended high up by wires in the centre of the roadways ; with the steam tramcars ; with the system of removing the snow by massing in the centre of the wider thoroughfares, and by emptying it down openings in the streets leading to the sewers below. We visited together the Museum of Egyptian antiquities —the inestimably valuable gatherings of the great Champollion : even Boulak scarcely possesses riches equal to those resulting from the labours of the indefatigable Frenchman. The day was a strict *festa*, and very few of the shops, other than those for the "restoration" of the inner man, were open. Still snowing! in some fear about our Alpine journey on the morrow.

January 7. We left the very pleasant city of Turin with some regret. One wanted to know more of the people and the place. Once upon a time it had been the capital of a kingdom, and the favourite home of a warlike race of kings ; now 'twas a provincial city, dependent no longer upon the king and the court. The mountains appeared very close to us as we sped on our way, but it was a long time before we really began our ascent. The route was most picturesque, and the ground—with its mantle of snow, and the drooping trees, covered with icicles and resplendent with frost sparkling like diamonds in the rays of the winter sun—was very pleasant to look upon. We entered the Mont Cenis Tunnel, that wonderful work of the Italian engineers, at 7 o'clock, and emerged into the dim light on the western side of the Alps in exactly twenty-seven minutes. We felt no inconvenience. The distance is nearly if not quite nine miles, but there was nothing to mark it out, save by its length, from any other tunnel through which we had passed. We supped at an Alpine village immediately after descending circuitously from the heights above, and then prepared for the long night which lay before us. We had no companions, and made ourselves exceedingly comfortable with the abundant wraps with which we were provided.

January 8. We reached *Paris* soon after 7 o'clock, where M. H. was received with all the honours by the agent of the Chatham and Dover Railway : our trouble was over : our luggage was taken in hand, and whether or not backsheesh was needed, I know not. All was carefully packed on the cab which took us to the Great Northern of France. We left soon after 8 o'clock, taking first a frugal but satisfying breakfast. Reached Calais at 1.30. I shared in the advantages that belong to the managership of the mighty railway over which my friend M. H. presides until the coming of the Ides of March ; lay on my back all the way in a luxurious deck cabin; bade defiance to the waters of the Channel, and reached, in splendid condition, the welcome shores of Old England in little more than an hour after leaving Calais pierhead. We left Dover about 3.30, and reached home at 6 o'clock. Thank God! Parted with much regret from my good friend Mortimer Harris. What a delightful compound the man is! Thoughtful and stern as a judge, yet bright and sparkling with infinite wit and humour ; a poet and a scholar, fond of old books and old world studies, yet alive to all that constitutes the life and literature of to-day ; as indifferent as a stoic, yet as loving as a woman ; looking upon the political party to which I belong, and to the politicians in whom I believe, with dislike, if not contempt, and with deadly hatred upon Jesuit priests and Popish perverts, yet bearing with me and having a pitying thought for even the "poor de'il" himself ; conducting with infinite skill the affairs of a great railway, yet believing, in his heart of hearts, that the world went wrong when the stage-coach and postchaise went out, and steam, telegraph, and telephone came in ; abusing his friends to their face, perhaps unjustly, yet resenting violently the most obvious truths if others utter them to their disparagement. How he would have chummed with Walter Savage Landor, sympathised with Sibthorp, and marched (if his gout permitted) with the Iron Duke to death and glory! When he heard that perhaps my diary might be printed, and if so would be dedicated to our mutual friend, J. M. C., he wrote some lines which I must add to my scribblings, that the first page which chronicles my respect for one friend, and the last which shows the poetic powers of the other, may at least give me that pleasure which no other part of my diary is likely to afford.

To J. M. C.

I HEAR, John M., that JUDD intends
    His tour in Egypt to relate,
    And the great work to dedicate
To you, the staunchest of his friends.

'Tis true, I hope—for we shall find
    In every page that he has writ
    The shrewd sound sense, the pregnant wit,
And treasures of his well-stored mind.

A style, whose smooth and lucid flow
    Can neither intermit nor fail,
    Will make the briefness of the tale
Its one and only fault, I know.

How he will paint us, one by one!
    Our little foibles he'll expose
    In bright and somewhat caustic prose,
But not in malice—only fun.

He'll do this as no other can.
    Yet through his observations keen,
    And pungent satire, will be seen
The kindly nature of the man.

I long to read what he will tell
    Of the adventures of his trip
    By rail, by donkey, and by ship,
And fellow travellers as well.

One point, at least, is clear. His pen
    Will there record that J. M. C.
    Throughout the world is known to be
A prince of tourists—and of men!

M. H.

www.ingramcontent.com/pod-product-compliance
Lightning Source LLC
Chambersburg PA
CBHW030339170426
43202CB00010B/1172